Xiphophorus variatus *(Variatus Platy)*

D0635678

A FISHKEEPER'S GUIDE TO

FISH BREEDING

Etroplus maculatus *(Orange Chromide) male guarding fry*

Papiliochromis ramirezi *(Ram or Butterfly Cichlid)*

A FISHKEEPER'S GUIDE TO

FISH BREEDING

Comprehensive advice on breeding and rearing a wide
selection of popular aquarium fishes

Dr Chris Andrews

Tetra🐟Press

No. 16066

A Salamander Book

© 1986 Salamander Books Ltd.,
52 Bedford Row,
London WC1R 4LR,
United Kingdom

ISBN 0 86101 209 7

This book may not be sold outside the United States of America.

All rights reserved. No part of this book
may be reproduced, stored in a retrieval system or transmitted
in any form or by any means, electronic, mechanical,
photocopying, recording or otherwise, without the
prior permission of Salamander Books Ltd.

All correspondence concerning the content of this book
should be addressed to Salamander Books Ltd.

Aequidens curviceps *(Flag Cichlid) spawning*

Credits

Editor: Geoff Rogers   Designer: Tony Dominy
Colour reproductions:
Rodney Howe Ltd.
Filmset: SX Composing Ltd.
Printed in Belgium by Henri Proost & Cie, Turnhout.

Author

Dr Chris Andrews is well known for his magazine articles and appearances on television in connection with the fishkeeping hobby. His interest in fish began with boyhood fishing trips to streams and ponds, and developed further as he kept a range of fish and other animals at home. After obtaining an Honours Degree in Zoology, he was awarded a Ph.D for his studies of fish diseases. He then spent eight years as a fisheries scientist for a Regional Water Authority and as consultant to a manufacturer of foods for the aquarium trade. In 1985, Dr Andrews took up the prestigious position of Assistant Curator (in charge of the Aquarium) at London Zoo, allowing his one-time hobby to become a challenging career.

Consultant

A practising fishkeeper, Dick Mills lectures widely to aquarist societies and is fully involved in the organisation of the hobby through the Federation of British Aquarist Societies. Dabbling in aquarium photography and writing books and articles take up the rest of his spare time away from his profession of composing electronic sounds and music for TV and radio programmes.

Contents

Introduction

Keeping fishes for ornamental purposes probably dates back to Roman times, although it was not until the first tropical fish (possibly the Paradisefish, *Macropodus opercularis*) was imported into Europe in the mid-1600s that the hobby started to become more widespread. During the intervening 1000 years or so, the keeping and selective breeding of Goldfish and Koi became very popular in China and Japan. With the opening up of trade and exploration routes around the world in the 18th and 19th centuries, a fascinating and hitherto unknown array of exotic fishes gradually became available to westerners. Jet air transport and, more recently, the commercial farming of ornamental fishes in places such as Singapore and Florida, have led to the present-day upsurge of interest in all aspects of the aquarium hobby. Now fishkeeping is a truly worldwide pursuit involving millions of enthusiasts.

Most fishkeepers begin by keeping a few tropical community

fishes in a small aquarium, or even Goldfishes in a simple bowl, but they soon want to find out more about how their fishes live – particularly how they breed. In the first section of this book, we look at some general aspects of fish breeding, including feeding, water chemistry, and pests and diseases. Careful selection of the 'brood stock', or potential parent fishes, is very important, as is their conditioning on a good varied diet and the maintenance of the correct water conditions. Attempting to breed fish that are too young or too old should be avoided, and careful consideration needs to be given to the availability of a suitable first food for the fry before they become free swimming.

The species section starting on page 38 looks in detail at the breeding of a wide selection of commonly kept aquarium fishes, and offers suitable encouragement for everyone interested in raising some of the more delicate, difficult-to-breed species.

General considerations

In the individual sections of Part Two, we look in detail at the aquarium breeding of a number of popular ornamental fishes. In this opening section, we cover a few points that apply to fish breeding in general, plus coping with common diseases.

Species selection
If you are a newcomer to the aquarium hobby, you are advised to begin your fish breeding attempts with easy-to-breed livebearers, such as guppies and platies (see page 96), before moving on to hardy egglayers, such as danios and barbs (see page 84). Armed with the experience gained in these initial endeavours, you can aspire to keep and breed other, perhaps more difficult species.

Selecting the parent fishes
Select the prospective parents, or 'brood fishes', for their good physical appearance, colour and finnage, as well as their health, vigour and willingness to feed. Preferably, select immature fishes, which you can grow on, or young mature fishes, which will be ready to breed with a small amount of 'conditioning'. These are much better choices than older fishes that may be nearing the end of their reproductive lives.

Avoid repeated interbreeding of parent fishes with their own offspring, and between brother and sister fishes. Although this technique is used in the selective breeding of certain features, so-called line breeding, it can lead to an increased occurrence of 'abnormal' fry. Introducing new brood fishes periodically is also recommended.

Of the species described in this book, some, such as livebearers and sticklebacks, can mature at just a few months of age. Depending on conditions, the majority probably mature at between 6 and 12 months, while others, such as goldfishes and sunfishes, usually mature at two to three years of age. Size alone can be deceiving, since small stunted fishes are often as 'mature' as larger individuals of the same age. If possible, however, try to avoid obviously stunted fishes when choosing brood stock.

Tank requirements
Although many fishes will breed successfully in a community tank of other fishes, a separate breeding tank often gives the best results. In fact, to breed many species successfully you will need a minimum of two tanks: one for breeding, and one in which to rear the fry or to allow one or both of the parent fishes to recuperate. Although buying extra breeding tanks may seem rather extravagant, these tanks will come in useful as necessary quarantine quarters when they are not needed for breeding purposes. Perforated tank dividers are also useful for quickly and easily converting one large tank into two or three smaller units.

Details on how to set up breeding and rearing tanks for individual fish species are provided in Part Two of the book. Fortunately, such tanks do not need to be very large and aquaria of 10-30 litres (2.2-6.6 gallons) will be adequate for most smaller fishes. Naturally, more spacious tanks of 50-100 litres (11-22 gallons) will be required for breeding larger fishes and for successfully rearing large broods of fry.

Keep decorations to a minimum in a breeding tank – just sufficient for the needs of the parent fishes and for the safety of the eggs and fry. While vigorous aeration and/or filtration is

Above and below: *Different fish species often require different tank conditions for breeding. Ideally, keep tank decorations to a minimum in breeding tanks. This helps with tank* *maintenance and good hygiene. Foam filters are excellent for most breeding tanks. They carry out biological and mechanical filtration, yet do not pose a threat to tiny fry.*

not usually needed in a breeding tank, for rearing fry provide a safe, efficient filter, such as a foam filter. Avoid over vigorous filtration, however, which may damage small fry.

When not in use, empty the breeding and rearing tanks, rinse them well in running water and store them dry together with all the

associated equipment until they are required again. To avoid transferring disease organisms between stock tanks and the breeding or rearing tanks, use a completely separate set of equipment (i.e. nets, buckets, siphon tubes, etc.) for the breeding operations. For general advice on tackling diseases see pages 30-37.

Feeding and breeding

We look at this subject in detail on page 24. Suffice it to say for the moment that a good varied diet is important for bringing adult fishes into breeding condition, and that the provision of a nutritious and suitably sized food is vital for the growth and well-being of the resultant fish fry. Avoid overfeeding; the golden rule of 'little and often' applies just as strictly to breeding as it does to more general aspects of fishkeeping.

Environmental influences

Fishes from temperate regions often display a marked seasonal periodicity in their breeding habits. Many species breed in the spring or early summer months, and increasing daylength and/or increasing water temperatures are thought to be important environmental 'triggers', essentially telling the fishes that the breeding season has arrived. Such environmental control ensures that the eggs and fry are produced at a time when water temperatures, plant cover and food availability are all optimal for their survival.

Therefore, for the controlled breeding of many 'coldwater' fishes under aquarium conditions, a seasonal variation in temperature and, perhaps, daylength may be important. Of course, in Europe and North America, most aquarium fish are usually more or less exposed to prevailing, and seasonally variable, daylength conditions. However, it may be unwise to maintain some coldwater fish in constant, warm conditions (i.e. at room temperature) throughout the year if fish breeding is your objective. This aspect is further explored from page 104 in relation to a number of coldwater species in which a winter decrease in temperature, followed by a spring temperature rise, is useful in

Above: *Angelfish prefer soft, slightly acid water for breeding, matching the water conditions in which they thrive in their South American home.*

Left: *A stretch of the River Amazon, in Peru. These waters are the home of Angelfish and many other tropical aquarium fishes that have become firm favourites throughout the world.*

stimulating them to breed.

In tropical regions, daylength and water temperatures fluctuate far less than they do in temperate regions, although there is often a marked seasonal periodicity in rainfall, with one or two pronounced annual peaks or 'wet seasons'.

The heavy, seasonal rains in the tropics obviously have a pronounced effect on the surrounding countryside – the level of the River Amazon at Manaus may rise by over 15m (50ft), for example – and this in turn can bring about a number of changes in the environment of the local fishes.

The rains may wash large amounts of vegetable matter and detritus into the pools, streams and rivers, introducing an abundance of live and other foods and causing extensive flooding. The latter effectively makes available to the fish new habitats that were once dry land. The heavy rainfall may also affect local water

conditions, slightly reducing temperature and, perhaps, pH level and water hardness. Factors such as these are important in signalling to the local fish populations that the wet season has begun, and that, for a period of several weeks, conditions are likely to be particularly favourable for breeding and for the survival of the subsequent eggs and fry.

As a result, while many tropical fish species may breed throughout the year, some show peaks in breeding activity in their tropical homes during the rainy season. Thus, live foods, the use of a 'blackwater tonic' (which contains various plant and peat extracts), and a discrete lowering of water temperature, pH and hardness may all be useful in inducing some tropical species to breed. Such factors are referred to in subsequent sections in relation to the needs of specific fishes and summarized in the form of breeding tables.

15

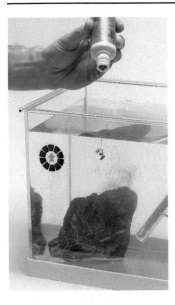

Above: *Using a 'blackwater tonic' helps to recreate the conditions that some egglaying fishes prefer. Note that such 'tonics' do not usually affect pH or hardness level, but add natural plant extracts to the water.*

Other controlling factors

While environmental factors, such as temperature and daylength, are very important influences controlling breeding in fishes, a number of other factors should not be overlooked. Chemical, sound or touch stimuli from fishes of the opposite sex, the presence of a suitable spawning medium, and the absence of a build-up of waste or other substances from the fish may all affect breeding success, or the lack of it. If conditions for breeding are not satisfactory, most fishes possess the ability to absorb the eggs or milt (sperm) they contain inside their bodies, and then to develop their breeding readiness again at a later time, when conditions in the environment improve.

Hormone injections

The induction of spawning in some comercially farmed food fishes, such as carp and catfishes, using hormone injections is now quite commonplace. This allows fish farmers to spawn the fishes at times of the year when they would otherwise not spawn, thus permitting a more constant availability of eggs and fry for growing on. The specially prepared hormone extract is injected into the fully matured brood fishes, and these are then either spawned by hand or allowed to spawn naturally, which usually happens within a few hours or a day or so. Obviously, this technique needs to be carried out by experienced people.

There is a considerable variation in the response to injected hormones between different fish species. Some will only react to hormones from their own or a closely related species, while in some catfishes, for example, mammalian hormones can be used.

Such methods have been used on a number of ornamental fishes, such as goldfish, koi, kuhli loach and freshwater 'sharks', and it is likely that further so-called 'difficult species' may eventually be bred using these techniques.

Outlets for the fish

Even if you are a novice fish breeder, you may soon find that you have more fishes than you can cope with. How do you dispose of the surplus stock?

Remove and painlessly destroy any deformed fry during their first few weeks of life. Unwanted healthy fishes can be disposed of in a number of ways, including selling or exchanging them at local fish club meetings or at your local aquarium dealer. Of course, well grown, colourful and perhaps less common fishes will be more sought after than small, poorly marked 'bread and butter' species.

Never release unwanted fishes of any kind into local ponds, streams or canals. Tropical species will not, of course, usually survive in temperate regions, although non-native coldwater species may not only establish, but breed and even compete with the local fish stocks. In addition, never release any non-native fishes into a natural water body, because of the risk of introducing previously non-existent fish disease organisms.

Keeping records

Hobbyists can do much to further our knowledge of the keeping and breeding of aquarium fishes. To this end, it is vital that you keep a written diary of any fish breeding attempts, recording failures as well as successes. Water conditions in the breeding tank, numbers of eggs or young, best fry foods, etc.; this is all information that other hobbyists will find useful. However, simply recording this information is not enough; make an effort to exchange your ideas and observations with the members of a local fish club, or by writing to one of the available hobbyist magazines.

Below: *The various factors involved in breeding fishes are summarized here in a logical sequence. Apply this general approach throughout.*

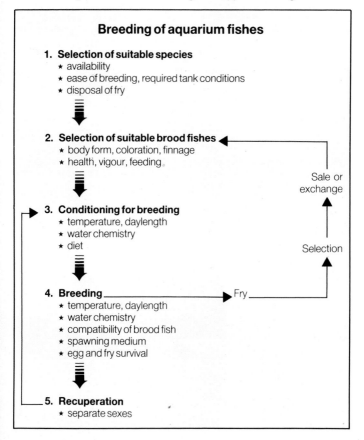

Breeding of aquarium fishes

1. **Selection of suitable species**
   - ★ availability
   - ★ ease of breeding, required tank conditions
   - ★ disposal of fry

2. **Selection of suitable brood fishes**
   - ★ body form, coloration, finnage
   - ★ health, vigour, feeding

3. **Conditioning for breeding**
   - ★ temperature, daylength
   - ★ water chemistry
   - ★ diet

4. **Breeding** —————————→ Fry
   - ★ temperature, daylength
   - ★ water chemistry
   - ★ compatibility of brood fish
   - ★ spawning medium
   - ★ egg and fry survival

5. **Recuperation**
   - ★ separate sexes

Sale or exchange

Selection

17

Water quality for breeding

In the sections dealing with breeding specific groups of fishes we lay considerable emphasis on providing the fishes with their preferred water conditions, particularly in terms of temperature, pH value and water hardness. Although the temperature of aquarium water is easy to monitor and keep within desired limits using a reliable heater-thermostat, the importance of pH value and water hardness is often overlooked or at least misunderstood.

The pH value of water

The pH value reflects the acidity or alkalinity of water, and is measured on a scale from 0 to 14. Pure water has a pH value of 7.0, and is said to be 'neutral'; more 'acid' water has a lower pH value, and more 'alkaline' water a higher pH value. An important point to remember here is that, since the pH scale is logarithmic, for each unit change in pH value there is a *ten-fold* change in the acidity or

alkalinity. Thus, what seems to be a small pH change to the aquarist can have a far more drastic effect on fishes, which can be sensitive to even small pH fluctuations.

Water hardness

Water hardness is related to the amounts of dissolved salts present in the water, and is measured by several different scales, including degrees of German hardness (°dH). The water hardness is actually made up of two components: the *general hardness* (or GH), which is related to the amounts of calcium and magnesium present, and the *carbonate hardness* (KH), which is related to the amounts of carbonate/bicarbonate present. Water with a hardness value of 3°dH or less is termed 'soft' (i.e. low in dissolved salts) and water with a hardness value of over 25°dH is termed 'very hard' (i.e rich in dissolved salts). The table opposite compares water hardness measured

―――――――――――― pH scale ――――――――――――

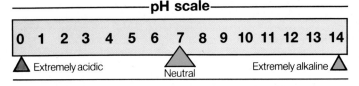

| 0 | 1 | 2 | 3 | 4 | 5 | 6 | 7 | 8 | 9 | 10 | 11 | 12 | 13 | 14 |

Extremely acidic   Neutral   Extremely alkaline

Above: *The acidity or alkalinity of water is measured on a pH scale from 0 to 14, but for each one unit change*

in pH there is a ten-fold change in acidity. Hence, pH in the aquarium must be altered very slowly.

Below: *To measure pH level using this test kit, simply add the required amount of reagent to a measured*

water sample and compare the colour change that results against a calibration chart provided with the kit.

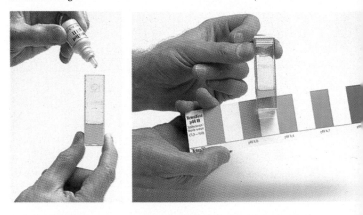

Water hardness in comparative terms

°dH	Mg/litre CaCO₃	Considered as
3	0-50	Soft
3-6	50-100	Moderately soft
6-12	100-200	Slightly hard
12-18	200-300	Moderately hard
18-25	300-450	Hard
Over 25	Over 450	Very hard

Several scales are used to express water hardness. Here, we compare the widely used German scale of °dH with an alternative scale based on milligrams of calcium carbonate (CaCO₃) per litre of water.

in °dH with an alternative scale based
on milligrams per litre of calcium
carbonate (mg/l CaCO₃). It is possible
to measure pH value and water
hardness easily and accurately using
the test kits widely available from
aquarium dealers.

Tapwater
Most aquarists rely, to a greater or
lesser extent, on tapwater to fill their
tanks. Tapwater is, of course,
intended for drinking rather than
fishkeeping, and a number of
problems can result if it is not first
conditioned before aquarium use.

In order to make the tapwater safe
and wholesome to drink, many water
authorities and companies add
chlorine as a means of destroying
potentially dangerous
microorganisms that might be
present. The level of chlorine in such
chlorinated water is harmless to
humans but can be toxic to fish.
Therefore, before using any tapwater

for fishkeeping, always remove the
chlorine, either by adding a suitable
tapwater conditioner, available from
aquarium dealers, or by allowing the
water to stand at room temperature
overnight, when the chlorine will
dissipate to the atmosphere.

Good quality tapwater conditioners
also exert a number of other beneficial
influences, including the removal of
heavy metals, such as copper, that
are potentially toxic for fish and fish
eggs. These can originate from the
water pipes in the house, and are a
particular problem in new houses or in
areas where the water is particularly
soft. If in doubt, test the water.

The pH value of tapwater is often
neutral to moderately alkaline
(pH 7.0-8.0), although the water
hardness values can vary
tremendously, depending on where
you live. While most fishes can survive
in quite a wide range of water
conditions, as long as extreme values
and sudden changes are avoided, a

Below: *This test for hardness entails
adding a reagent to a water sample
and counting the number of drops*

*needed to cause a colour change.
The number of drops equals the
number of degrees hardness (°dH).*

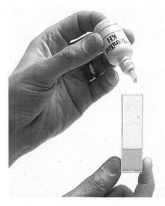

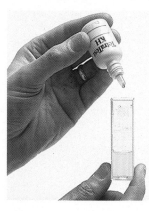

Above: *Always condition fresh tapwater before using it for fishkeeping. Good conditioners do more than just remove chlorine.*

number of the popular aquarium species prefer soft, slightly acid water, especially for breeding.

Tapwater can usually be made more acid by allowing it to stand in contact with aquarium peat for one to two weeks or so before use. Allow about two handfuls of aquarium peat, loosely tied in a fine mesh bag (an old stocking will do), for every 10-15 litres (2.2-3.3 gallons) of water. Measure the pH value of this water before using it in the aquarium, remembering that fish are quite sensitive to sudden changes in pH value of more than 0.5 unit. A pH value of about 5.0 is the lowest safe limit for most fishes preferring more acidic conditions.

Very hard water may not respond to this type of acidification, but it can be softened first by dilution with clean rainwater, which itself can also be quite acid. In industrial areas, the rainwater may also be rather polluted. This can be offset by collecting the rainwater in a continuously overflowing water butt, which serves to dilute any pollutants present.

In order to determine the relative amounts of tapwater and rainwater needed to achieve a desired hardness, carry out one or two small scale experiments (in the absence of fish), or follow the guidelines in the 'Pearson square' shown opposite.

With practice, it is possible to become quite proficient at softening the water and reducing its pH value in one go by allowing aquarium peat to stand in contact with a mixture of the desired amounts of tapwater and rainwater. Of course, always monitor any such modifications of water quality using reliable test kits.

Some aquarists prefer to use 'ion exchangers' to produce soft water for aquarium use. The typical domestic water softener is probably not really suitable for fishkeeping purposes. Such water softeners exchange 'hard' calcium and magnesium for 'soft' sodium, and hence, while the water 'feels' soft, it contains what may be to some fish unsatisfactorily high levels of sodium.

Using a two-stage demineralisation water softener is probably better for aquarium use. These water softeners are based on disposable cartridges that remove calcium, magnesium *and* carbonate/bicarbonate from

Amount of soft and hard water needed to achieve water of a desired hardness.

"Pearson Square or St. Andrews Cross"

Assume tapwater to have a general hardness of 16°dH, the available rainwater or softened water to have a general hardness of 0°dH, and the desired general hardness to be 2°dH.

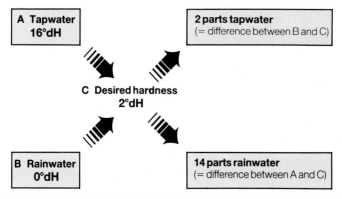

A Tapwater 16°dH	2 parts tapwater (= difference between B and C)

C Desired hardness 2°dH

B Rainwater 0°dH	14 parts rainwater (= difference between A and C)

Above: *This simple calculation allows you to estimate the amount of 'hard' and 'soft' water required to create water of the desired hardness.*

tapwater, and produce water which is very pure indeed. However, be sure to allow the water to stand overnight and then mix it with a little hard tapwater before using it in the aquarium. Water straight from this type of softening device is really too pure for fishkeeping, and subject to pH instability. However, mixed with a little tapwater, it can be used to produce aquarium water of the desired hardness value.

Always remember to carry out one or two trials, in the absence of fishes, whenever you make alterations to aquarium water. And never expose fishes to sudden marked changes in water quality, especially in terms of temperature and pH value.

Ammonia and nitrite problems
The natural processes of the nitrogen cycle convert nitrogen-containing waste products from the fish,

Below: *Brown, peaty water is often soft and acidic. The same effect can be achieved for fish breeding by using rainwater and aquarium peat.*

uneaten food and plant fragments into ammonia (NH_3), then nitrite (NO_2), and eventually nitrate (NO_3). Ammonia and nitrite are more toxic to fish than nitrate, and nitrate is used by plants as a food source. This sequence of chemical processes is made possible by the activities of various helpful bacteria, and forms the basis of biological filtration used in, for example, the commonly available undergravel and foam filters.

In newly established tanks, however, only small numbers of these helpful bacteria are present, and until their numbers build up – which can take several weeks – quite high levels of ammonia and nitrite can be recorded, resulting in the well-known 'new tank syndrome' losses.

Once the tank and its filtration system are established, a number of factors can adversely affect the normal efficient running of the nitrogen cycle – including shortage of oxygen, chemical treatment and low pH value of the water – and perhaps cause at least temporary peaks of toxic ammonia and nitrite.

Below: *This graph shows the changes in water quality during the six to eight weeks after an aquarium has been set up. Two or three weeks after introducing fishes, the level of ammonia reaches a maximum (A). As this falls, nitrite reaches a peak after three to six weeks (B), followed by a gradually increasing nitrate level (C). The nitrate level may take several months to increase noticeably and can usually be reduced by regular partial water changes.*

In order for the helpful filter bacteria to function properly, they must be continuously provided with well-oxygenated water. Thus, filters carrying out biological filtration should be left running for most of the time, although occasionally turning them off for an hour or so will not cause too much harm. Since such filters usually become clogged with accumulated debris as time passes, their regular cleaning is important for long-term, efficient filtration. To maintain the gravel beds of an undergravel filter in good condition, 'hoover' it regularly using a siphon tube or clean it using an in-tank 'gravel washer'. Rinse the cartridges of foam filters in water at aquarium temperature every 2-4 weeks, before slipping them back on to their filter tubes.

Certain disease treatments, such as some antibiotics and methylene blue, also adversely affect the non-disease producing bacteria in the filter. Therefore, do not use disease treatments in a heavily stocked tank that relies on biological filtration unless you know it is safe to do so. Fortunately, many of the proprietary brands of disease treatments available today have been developed for use in the aquarium without harming the filter bacteria.

The bacteria responsible for converting ammonia to nitrite and then nitrate function best in warm, neutral to alkaline water, and they do not carry out their task particularly well in cool, acid water, i.e. at less than 10-15°C (50-59°F) and with a pH value lower than 7.0. Consequently, keep a close check on ammonia and

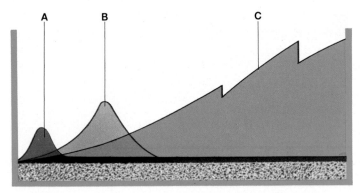

A　　　　B　　　　　　　　　　C

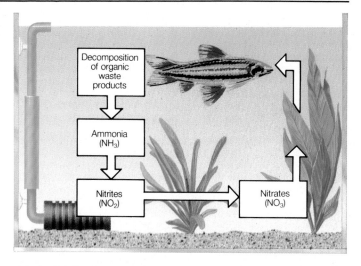

Boxes in diagram:
Decomposition of organic waste products → Ammonia (NH_3) → Nitrites (NO_2) → Nitrates (NO_3)

nitrite levels in heavily stocked rearing tanks containing coldwater fishes or acid-loving species, such as discus. In such situations, make regular partial water changes and/or use zeolite compounds to absorb ammonia to ensure stable water conditions.

In an established, well-maintained aquarium, there should be little or no ammonia and/or nitrite. Ammonia or nitrite levels of 0.2mg/l, or above, should be viewed with some suspicion. In fact, ammonia is particularly toxic to fish in alkaline water with a pH value above 8.0, and therefore take particular care with tanks containing, for example, Rift Valley cichlids or marine fishes.

Regular water quality monitoring, sensible filter maintenance, and frequent partial water changes, plus 'hoovering' the tank floor, are all recommended, especially in heavily stocked rearing tanks. And be sure to avoid overfeeding; the accumulation of uneaten food is another potential source of ammonia/nitrite problems in the aquarium.

Fluctuating pH levels
In an established, well-planted freshwater community tank, it is not uncommon for the pH value to gradually rise, i.e. for the water to become more alkaline. This is caused principally by the plants extracting carbon dioxide from the water for

Above: *Useful bacteria convert ammonia from fish wastes and uneaten food to nitrite and then to nitrate. This is the naturally occurring 'nitrogen cycle'. Since these bacteria require oxygen to survive, leave biological filters running for 20-24 hours a day once established and maintain them regularly.*

photosynthesis. However, the pH value of the water rarely rises to a dangerous level for the fish, and the increase is normally kept in check by partial water changes.

Certain fish species need quite soft water for breeding purposes. Such soft water has a low carbonate hardness (KH) value, and hence has little 'buffering' capacity. Water with little buffering capacity can be subject to sudden pH fluctuations, which in an unplanted or lightly planted breeding or rearing tank are likely to cause a sudden fall in pH value to a dangerously acid level.

In breeding and rearing tanks containing such soft (or low KH) water, be sure to monitor the pH level regularly using a reliable test kit. It is possible to exercise some control over the pH level by adding small amounts of a proprietary buffer solution or pH adjuster to the tank. Always carry out small scale sighting experiments, however, before adding such chemicals to a tank containing fish. And read instructions carefully.

Feeding for breeding

Aquarium fish are dependent upon the aquarist to provide them with a correct balanced diet, the overall effects of which will be seen in their coloration, growth, resistance to disease and their willingness to breed. Today, a balanced diet for aquarium fish is most easily and conveniently provided by using the high-quality flaked and similar prepared diets that are available from pet and aquatic dealers. Such foods have now largely replaced the old-fashioned, inconvenient and often potentially dangerous home-made and live foods that were so popular 20 or 30 years ago.

However, live foods do still have a number of specific uses in fishkeeping, and these include:

1 Tempting delicate, fussy fish on to feed, before weaning them on to a prepared diet.

2 Conditioning adult fish for breeding, perhaps by an abundance of live food acting as a 'trigger' to initiate spawning.

3 Providing a useful first food for newly hatched fish fry, before they can take finely powdered dried foods.

Using live foods brings with it a number of potential dangers. To begin with, feeding a limited number of types of live foods to the exclusion of all other kinds of foods is unlikely to provide the fish with a balanced diet, and may even lead to nutritional or other internal disorders. Furthermore, many live foods come from ponds, streams or rivers, and may bring with them aquarium pests, such as *Hydra*, snails, etc., or fish disease organisms. The risk of introducing fish disease organisms can be reduced by collecting live foods from fish-free environments – but the possibility of introducing aquarium pests still remains – or by using live foods of terrestrial origin.

Here is a selection of live foods that you are likely to find useful for breeding fish. Information on their collection, storage and/or culture is provided, along with hints on how you may best use them in the aquarium.

Brineshrimp
There can be few aquarists who have bred and raised fish who have not heard of the Brineshrimp (*Artemia salina*). This tiny saltwater crustacean is frequently used as a food for newly hatched fish fry and it is still the main standby for carp farmers rearing newly hatched fish through their first few days of life.

Brinshrimp eggs are available from most pet stores. However, it is sometimes a false economy to buy in bulk. If stored under unsatisfactory conditions, the hatchability of the eggs may decrease markedly with time. Ideally, the eggs should be stored in cool, dry conditions.

Culturing brineshrimp is relatively easy. You can buy a 'brineshrimp hatchery' from a pet store, although in the short-term it is just as easy to get good results by using several clean glass bottles or jars.

Set up the 'bottle hatchery' in a warm room. The temperature should be at least 15°C (59°F), although the eggs will hatch more quickly (within 24-48 hours) if maintained at a temperature of 20-25°C (68-77°F).

Add approximately half a litre (about three-quarters of a pint) of cooled, boiled water to one of the

Below: *A spotlamp can be used to attract crustacean live foods, such as brineshrimp and* Daphnia. *Concentrated in the narrow beam, the fish can find them more easily.*

Above: *Brineshrimp are easy to culture in clean glass bottles, although proper 'brineshrimp hatcheries' are available. Warm, saline and well-aerated water is essential for successful brineshrimp culture. Siphon off the crustaceans after 24-48 hours and aerate the culture again for a new 'harvest'.*

bottles and into this dissolve about 10-15gm (a heaped teaspoonful) of cooking salt, although a better percentage hatch may be obtained if you use marine salts. Aerate and allow this solution to reach room temperature. Then add a 'pinch' of brineshrimp eggs to the salt water. The aeration must be quite vigorous and it is probably a good idea to place a cotton wool bung in the neck of the bottle or jar. For a successful hatch, the eggs must be kept in *warm*, *saline* and *well-aerated* water.

One or two days after starting the first culture, set up a second bottle, followed by a third after another couple of days. The eggs will hatch after about 24-48 hours, and starting several cultures in succession will guarantee the availability of newly hatched brineshrimp over a week or so. By this time, most fish should accept finely powdered dried foods.

In the bottle culture the newly hatched brineshrimp may be separated from the egg shells and unhatched eggs by turning off the aeration for a few minutes. The living brineshrimp will collect in a layer

about 2.5-5cm (1-2in) from the bottom of the bottle and may be siphoned out using a piece of air line. Top up the bottle with dechlorinated, saline water and turn on the aeration again. Each culture should last for two or three days.

A commercially prepared food for brineshrimp is now available, making it possible to rear on newly hatched crustaceans for feeding to larger fish, particularly marines.

Whiteworms
These worms of the *Enchytraeus* genus are approximately 0.5-1cm (0.2-0.4in) long and are an excellent live food – whether chopped and fed to small fish or fed whole to larger fish. Starter cultures are available from most pet stores and whiteworms are quite easy to culture in a shallow box with a tight-fitting lid.

Fill the box about three-quarters full with a good loamy garden soil. It may be necessary to add aquarium peat to a clay soil. The main objective is to choose an organically rich soil that will retain moisture. Just before adding the starter culture, spray the soil so that it is well moistened but not waterlogged. Add the starter culture and then a little moistened white bread, pre-cooked porridge or baby breakfast cereal as food. Place the lid on the box and store the culture in the dark at about 15-20°C (59-68°F). Provide ventilation for the culture by way of small air holes in the sides of the box or in the lid.

Above: *Whiteworms can be cultured in a ventilated box of good moist soil with cereal or bread as food.*
Below: *Separate the worms from the food and soil in some water.*

Inspect the culture from time to time, paying particular attention to the moisture content. If the soil dries out, the worms will be unable to survive. But do not overfeed the culture; the uneaten food may 'sour' the culture and allow pests to flourish. Experience will indicate the correct amount of food to be provided; as a guide each new batch of food should be eaten within two or three days. Remove any uneaten food as you add fresh supplies.

Spread out the food in small pieces; the whiteworms will collect directly beneath these islands and be easy to remove with forceps. If it proves difficult to separate the worms from the food or soil, simply place a spoonful of the 'mix' in a saucer and cover it with water. The worms should migrate outwards and be easy to collect for immediate use.

Within about a month of setting up the culture in acceptable conditions, the population of whiteworms should approximately double. Within two months, a single culture should be providing enough worms for a reasonable collection of fishes.

Other, even smaller Enchytraeid worms, such as microworms and grindalworms, can be cultured in the same way and form a valuable first food for many growing fishes.

Earthworms
An excellent and often overlooked live food is the common earthworm. Although you can buy these from some pet stores and angling tackle dealers, if you have access to a garden, allotment or patch of waste ground then you should be able to collect more than a sufficient supply for your fishes. In damp weather, simply dig them up, or pick them up when they come to the surface of the lawn after an evening shower of rain in the summer. In dry weather, place one or two damp sacks in a shady part of the garden and 'bait' them with some potato peelings or similar vegetable scraps about once a week. You will also find an abundant supply of earthworms around manure heaps in farms or stables.

After collection, keep the earthworms for a few days in a sealed container – with small air holes for ventilation – containing a little damp grass or moss. During this time, they will 'clean' themselves of soil etc., and will then be more palatable to the fish. You can use earthworms whole or chopped, depending on their size and the size of fishes you are feeding.

Infusorians
Infusorians are tiny single-celled animals that abound in almost every body of water. They form an ideal first food for very tiny fish fry. They are easy to culture in large jars. To ensure a continuous supply, start a new culture every three or four days, until the fry will take a proprietary liquid fry food, brineshrimp or finely powdered dried foods.

To a jar three-quarters filled with boiled, cooled tapwater, add three or four bruised lettuce leaves, a whole banana skin, or even a little hay which has had boiling water poured over it to break up the cells. Place the jar in a warm, moderately lit place with the lid off. Over the ensuing few days the culture should go cloudy and begin to smell slightly. Then it will clear as the infusorians develop. Once the culture is clear and 'sweet smelling', pour or siphon it into the tank a little at a time.

Obviously, it is important to time the availability of the infusorians to coincide with the fry 'coming on to

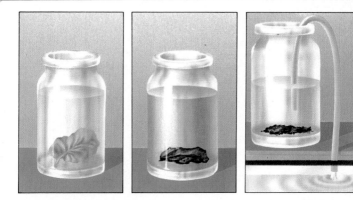

feed', and then to maintain a satisfactory supply until the small fish can readily accept proprietary brands of prepared diets.

Sludge worms

Tubifex and other similar tubificid worms are a familiar form of live food. These slim, maroon worms, about 1cm (0.4in) long, are useful for tempting fish such as discus on to feed, and as a live food for adult breeding fish. *Tubifex* is not easy to culture, however, and so it is best to buy supplies as you need them from your local aquatic store.

Unfortunately, in the wild these worms abound in the bottom mud of rather polluted stretches of rivers and streams, and it is from these unsavoury sources that most *Tubifex* worms for aquarium use are derived.

Below: *Use* Tubifex *worms carefully in the aquarium. They may introduce pests and diseases and must be rinsed in clean water before use.*

Above: *Infusorians can be cultured in glass jars, and then siphoned into the fry tank. These single-celled organisms are useful as a first food for tiny fish fry. As the fry grow, they can be weaned on to brineshrimp, and liquid or dried prepared fry foods.*

Therefore, use *Tubifex* sparingly in the aquarium, and as an occasional food rather than a staple diet. Before use, gently rinse the worms in cold, running tapwater for several hours, and perhaps give a preventative treatment with one of the liquid food disinfectants available from aquatic stores. Once cleaned, you can keep *Tubifex* worms alive for some time in a shallow dish of cold water, flushing it through with fresh water every day.

Water fleas

Water fleas are tiny planktonic crustaceans such as *Daphnia* and *Cyclops*. Like *Tubifex*, they are a popular live food among aquarists. You can either buy them in small plastic bags from an aquatic store or collect them with a fine hand net from a local pond in the summer months, when they 'bloom' rather like algae in a garden pond.

However, and also like *Tubifex*, using water fleas as an aquarium live food may result in the introduction of unwanted pests or disease organisms. Unfortunately, *Daphnia* and the like are less easily 'disinfected' than *Tubifex*. Thus, be sure to collect water fleas for aquarium use from a fish-free pond, or culture them from known disease-free stock. For culturing *Daphnia*, use an old aquarium or plastic tub containing about 20 or 30 litres (4.4-6.6 gallons) of tapwater that has been allowed to stand for 24-48 hours. Before adding the 'starter culture' of water fleas – obtained from a local aquarium store or 'safe' pond – fertilize the water with a handful or so of stable manure tied loosely in a nylon bag. This will cause the water to go slightly cloudy after a week or so, which signifies that the microorganisms on which the *Daphnia* feed have started to build up to a useful level.

Now add the *Daphnia* starter culture, and over the ensuing few weeks their numbers will increase so that you can cull them, using a fine meshed net, several times a week to feed to larger fish fry or to condition adult fish for spawning. At any one time, do not remove more than about 20 percent of the *Daphnia* for feeding purposes, since this may deplete the culture beyond recovery.

The manure should provide sufficient nutrients to feed the water fleas for several weeks, after which time you should replace it with a new supply. Bakers' yeast is another form of food for *Daphnia*; add this in small amounts several times a week, taking

Above: *Remove uneaten food with a siphon to prevent tank pollution. Careful feeding also avoids a build up of excess food in the tank.*

great care to avoid overfeeding and fouling the culture. Adding the occasional lettuce leaf to the culture also seems to help.

You can culture *Daphnia* outdoors in plastic or glass covered containers during the warmer months of the year, although they will go dormant during the winter. Alternatively, culture *Daphnia* indoors at a

Below: *A varied diet is important for successful fish breeding. Live foods have advantages and disadvantages; choose and use them wisely.*

Live foods and breeding

Conditioning foods for adult fishes	Fry foods
Whiteworm	Infusorians
Chopped earthworms	Brineshrimp
Water fleas	Sieved water fleas
Tubifex	
Bloodworm	
Feed sparingly, perhaps several times a week	Feed fish fry several times a day, avoiding tank pollution, yet checking that the fry have full, rounded bellies
Use prepared foods as a staple diet, given sparingly two or three times a day	Wean on to powdered dry foods and other prepared diets as soon as practical, so as to maximize the growth rate of the fry

Safe live foods

Food	Source	Culture method	Suitable for
Infusorians	Bruised lettuce leaves, banana skins, hay, etc	In jars of water and a little vegetable/organic matter. Keep at a warm room temperature in a well-lit spot	Very small fish fry
Brineshrimp	Eggs from dealer	Eggs hatch in aerated, saline water at 15-25°C (59-77°F) after about 48 hours. Start successive cultures on alternate days	Most fish fry. (Brineshrimp can be reared on for bigger fishes)
Whiteworm	Starter culture from dealer	Shallow box with tight fitting lid, threequarters full of loamy soil. Feed on bread, breakfast cereal, etc. Keep moist at 15-20°C (59-68°F). Avoid overfeeding culture and drying out	Small to medium-sized fishes
Earthworms	Garden	Not necessary. Maintain a supply beneath damp sacks in a shady part of the garden	Small to very large fish

Above: *The live foods listed here are safer to use than others, as they are less likely to introduce pests and diseases into the aquarium.*

temperature of about 20°C (68°F) and with some overhead illumination. This will provide a supply of live food through most of the year.

Bloodworms
Bloodworms are the aquatic larval stage of a two-winged fly. Difficult for the aquarist to culture, they are often available from aquatic stores. They are particularly useful in the winter months, when other live foods may be scarce. Since they come from an aquatic environment, the above-mentioned risks also apply to the use of bloodworms. However, used sparingly, they can help to bring some fish into breeding condition.

In summary, despite the risks and inconveniences associated with their use, live foods still have a number of specific uses in the aquarium, particularly for breeding and rearing fish. However, do not use such foods to replace the more convenient, safe and high-quality prepared diets now available. And, wherever possible, use the safe live foods, such as earthworms, brineshrimp, whiteworm and infusorians, in preference to the potentially more dangerous live foods collected from natural aquatic sources.

Diseases, pests and problems

While breeding the fishes featured in this book is certainly within the capabilities of most fishkeepers, such endeavours are not, from time to time, without problems. Here we review the common diseases, pests and miscellaneous problems that may arise in the aquarium.

Infectious diseases
Fish are, of course, susceptible to a huge range of parasites and infectious diseases, the overall effects of which are increased by overcrowding and/or poor aquarium care. A number of these infections are of particular significance to the amateur fish breeder.

White spot disease is caused by the protozoan parasite *Ichthyophthirius*, which has a direct fish-to-fish life cycle, and can hence build up quickly within the confines of a well-stocked aquarium. It is relatively easy to diagnose, as it appears as small, white pimples about the size of a sugar grain on the skin, fins and gills of fish. Heavily infected fishes will scrape against rocks in an irritated fashion, and may suffer from secondary fungal or bacterial infections.

White spot is usually introduced into an aquarium along with new fishes, or with live foods or plants. Thus, quarantining all new fishes for

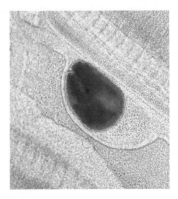

Above: *White spot parasites can occur on the gills of apparently healthy fish, highlighting the need to quarantine and treat all new fishes.*

two weeks – along with a preventative treatment using a proprietary brand of white spot remedy – is always recommended for all potential brood stock. In addition, use only safe live foods (as described on page 29). Also be sure to give all plants a good rinse in clean water before placing them in an aquarium containing fishes. Fortunately, there are a number of safe, effective white spot treatments

Below: *The characteristic appearance of white spot. Since the parasite can multiply rapidly in warm conditions, prompt treatment is vital.*

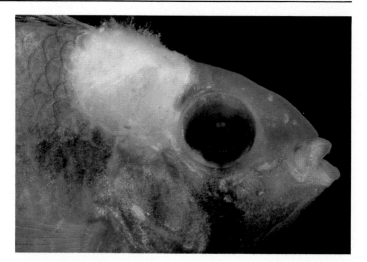

available from aquarium stores, and prompt treatment when the first 'spots' appear usually brings the disease under control.

Sliminess of the skin is caused by heavy infestations of tiny parasites such as *Chilodonella*, trichodinids, and *Gyrodactylus* which irritate the skin of the fish host, causing it to scratch against rocks and the aquarium gravel, and to increase mucus production – giving the skin a slimy, grey appearance. Fortunately, one or two treatments in the aquarium with a proprietary white spot remedy (or a similar broad-spectrum anti-parasite chemical) usually bring the problem under control. Newly imported fishes and coldwater fishes in the spring often suffer from this disease. In common with white spot, the parasites that cause 'sliminess of the skin' can rapidly build up to disease proportions in a heavily stocked tropical aquarium.

Fungus, such as *Saprolegnia* and *Achyla*, is a common disease among aquarium fishes, although it usually only affects fishes that are already in poor condition for some other reason. The spores, or 'seeds', that give rise to the fungal infection are extremely common in water, but can only penetrate the skin of fishes that have been damaged by rough handling,

Above: *The white, cotton-wool-like tufts of fish fungus, which can also affect fish eggs. Adding a treatment to the tank is the best strategy.*

fighting, spawning activity, or attack by other parasites.

If left untreated, the off-white or grey cotton-wool-like fungal growth can spread rapidly across the body of the fish, eventually killing it. Consequently, prompt treatment with a proprietary brand of fungus remedy is recommended.

Fish eggs are also susceptible to fungal attack. It is usually the dead, opaque-white eggs that succumb first, but if left untreated, the infection can then spread to live eggs. Carefully remove the dead, infected eggs using a razor blade and/or eye-dropper, and treat the remaining eggs with a proprietary brand of fungus treatment safe for use on fish eggs.

'Mouth fungus', which is caused by the bacterium *Flexibacter* often occurs in recently imported fishes, or those kept in unhygienic conditions. Mollies and certain other livebearers seem particularly prone to the disease. If tackled promptly, outbreaks of 'mouth fungus' usually respond to treatment with the proprietary remedies available from aquatic stores. More 'difficult' cases can usually be successfully treated with antibiotics supplied by a veterinarian used to treating fishes.

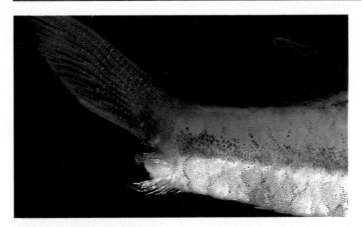

Above: *Fin rot is usually related to a localized bacterial infection, which may be brought on by poor aquarium conditions or fighting.*

Fin rot is usually the result of a localized bacterial infection, brought on by fighting or fin-nipping, overcrowding, poor diet or generally unhygienic tank conditions. The fins appear split and ragged, and may be streaked with blood or show reddening at the fin bases. As with all diseases, prompt treatment is important, and there are a number of proprietary brands of general fish tonics that are active against fin rot.

Both fin rot and fungus can be vital indicators that conditions are less than satisfactory in the breeding or rearing tank, and require immediate attention from the aquarist.

Systemic bacterial infections throughout the body of the fish often manifest themselves as ulcers, reddened areas on the body, and reddening at the vent and fin bases, together with listless behaviour and loss of appetite. Such infections may be brought on by incorrect tank conditions, although newly imported and recently spawned fish are also particularly susceptible.

Isolate fish showing signs of this disease from apparently unaffected fishes, and treat them by feeding an antibiotic medicated flaked food or by adding antibiotics to the water (under veterinary supervision). Large aquarium fishes can be injected with

a suitable antibiotic preparation, although this, too, must be carried out with the cooperation of a veterinarian. Once the symptoms subside, and a treated fish begins behaving normally, return it to the stock tank.

Since recently imported fishes are particularly susceptible to this problem, quarantine all new fishes and keep a close watch on them for any telltale signs of disease. Such measures should prevent an outbreak in the stock tank.

Hole-in-the-head disease often affects discus fishes, oscars and other cichlids, as well as gouramis. It is caused by unsatisfactory tank conditions, poor diet or the stress resulting from spawning, activating low-level infections with the protozoan *Hexamita* (or *Octomitis*). The result is the appearance of typical shallow, pale, crater-like lesions in the head and lateral line region, with coincident listless behaviour, pale, stringy faeces and an emaciated appearance.

Isolate affected fishes and treat them with suitable drugs available from a veterinarian or by adding a proprietary remedy to the water of the treatment tank. At the same time, improve general conditions in the stock tank, especially hygiene, and offer all the fishes a nutritious, varied diet (see pages 24-29).

Many other infectious diseases can affect fishes, although most can be prevented by providing suitable tank

 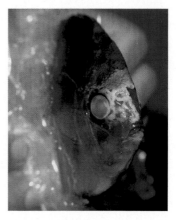

Above: *Ulcer disease is caused by a systemic bacterial infection and should be treated with antibiotics supplied by a veterinarian.*

Above: *Typical 'hole-in-the-head' symptoms in an Oscar. Infection can also develop in other cichlids and gouramis. Use a proprietary remedy.*

conditions, which include regularly changing part of the tank water and servicing the filters, and by feeding a good varied diet.

Neon Tetra disease, which affects a range of fish and not just Neons, is caused by the unicellular sporozoan parasite *Pleistophora*. Common in newly imported fishes kept in unhygienic conditions, its passage from fish to fish may be aided by cannibalism in overcrowded tanks. Symptoms usually include a loss of colour and general lethargy, although coincident wasting and loss of appetite may indicate fish tuberculosis (i.e. infestation with *Mycobacterium*). Both Neon Tetra disease and fish TB are difficult to control and once either disease has taken hold, there is no reliable treatment. Tank disinfection and refurbishment, along wih restocking from an alternative source may be necessary. In establshed aquariums, the prompt removal of dead and dying fish, vigorous power filtration and regular 'hoovering' of the tank floor may help control an outbreak of both diseases.

Treating for disease
Most good aquatic stores should stock a range of treatments suitable for combating the diseases that commonly affect tropical aquarium fishes. Be sure to choose a treatment that comes with full instructions for use, together with details of its active ingredients. Follow the instructions closely, and remember that filtration using activated carbon, and large amounts of organic matter in the tank, will reduce the effectiveness of most treatments. Above all, remember that prevention is better than cure.

Pests
Here we look at common pests that may present a hazard to your fish-breeding plans.

Snails are by no means an essential part of a tropical or coldwater aquarium and since some species may develop to pest proportions, it is best to prevent their introduction into a tank if at all possible. A basic preventative measure is to rinse *all* plants in running water before adding them to a set-up or breeding tank.

Control measures include:
1 Introducing fish such as the Clown Loach and other *Botia* species, Opaline Gouramis, Convict Cichlids or Puffer Fish, which will feed on some snails found in aquaria.
2 Placing one or two fish food tablets beneath an upturned saucer on the tank floor and leaving it overnight. The

33

snails will be attracted by the tablets and may be removed with the saucer the next morning. You will probably need to repeat this process every night for a week or so. Do not allow uneaten tablets to pollute the tank.
3 Chemical snail-eradicators exist, but be sure to use these carefully, especially in a badly infested tank.

Even when present in large numbers, snails are unsightly rather than dangerous to fish. If all else fails, you may need to strip the tank down completely, rinse all the rocks, gravel and decorations in dilute bleach or formalin – followed by a good rinse in clean water – and dip all the plants in a cherry-red solution of potassium permanganate for a few minutes.

Hydra – small freshwater anemone-like creatures – are often introduced into the aquarium with live food. Up to 2.5cm (1in) long when extended, their bodies will contract when disturbed, thus masking their characteristic many tentacled appearance. Using the tiny stinging cells in their tentacles, *Hydra* prey on live food, small fish and fish fry in the aquarium.

Control measures include:
1 Introducing fishes, such as gouramis or Paradisefish (*Macropodus opercularis*), that will prey on *Hydra*.
2 Using a six-volt battery. Connect two pieces of insulated copper wire to the battery, one to each terminal, and strip the insulation from the other ends of the wire for several centimetres and hang these bare ends in the tank. Left in the tank for three to six hours, this should bring about the death of most of the *Hydra*, probably by copper poisoning. Immediately afterwards, carry out a 25-50 percent water change and remove all the dead *Hydra* using a siphon tube. Do not use tapwater conditioners in an aquarium for a few days before using this type of treatment to eradicate *Hydra*.

Flatworms, bristleworms and one or two other similar pests are often introduced into the aquarium with live food and they then thrive in unhygienic, dirty conditions. Uneaten

Above: *Hydra can paralyze tiny fish fry using stinging cells on their tentacles. Food captured by the tentacles is drawn into the central column, which acts as a distensible 'stomach' with a digestive action. Hydra are normally introduced into the tank with live food or plants.*

food and accumulated organic matter are a great encouragement to such pests. Rather like snails, these pests are unsightly rather than harmful, although they may attack fish eggs and fry.

Control measures include:
1 Eliminate overfeeding, increase partial water changes, remove any accumulated debris, wash all plants before introducing them, ensure regular filter maintenance.
2 Introduce fish, such as gouramis, Siamese Fighting Fish or Kribensis, to feed on these pests, particularly flatworms.
3 Remove all fish and raise the tank temperature to 35°C (95°F) for several hours. This will kill flatworms, although a partial water change and a reduction in temperature will be necessary before the fish can be reintroduced into the aquarium.
If, however, all else fails, strip down and refurbish the tank as described for eradicating snails.

Above: *White, opaque eggs with fungus will infect nearby healthy eggs if not treated or removed. Eggs may not develop properly because the brooding pair are immature or the eggs are not fertilized.*

Miscellaneous problems

On occasion, fish may spawn repeatedly, yet the eggs never develop and hatch, but simply turn white and/or develop fungus. This can be related to a number of factors, including immaturity of the breeding pair – especially the male – and

Below: *Use a gently bubbling airstone to ensure the passage of water over developing eggs. This can be important when some cichlid eggs are reared away from the fanning given by the parent fishes.*

incorrect sexing of the two fishes, with two females being used rather than a true pair. Separating the fishes and conditioning them on a good varied diet may help them to become fully mature, or exchanging one of the 'pair' for a known male fish are possible solutions to this problem. Naturally, water quality conditions in the affected tank should be checked against the requirements of the species being bred.

Even when provided with seemingly ideal conditions for breeding, some fish will refuse to spawn. In this situation, the sex and, as far as is possible, the maturity of the would-be parents should be checked, and the fishes separated for further 'conditioning' (see page 17) before reintroduction. Nonetheless, some fish – especially certain cichlids, it seems – will not breed with just any member of the opposite sex, and hence exchanging one of the two partners may bring about the desired results. Natural selection of pairs, from a number of young fishes raised together, will ensure better results.

Some fish, such as many characins and barbs, are notorious egg eaters,

Below: *Methylene blue is a popular, if somewhat old-fashioned, treatment to prevent egg fungus. Here, it provides Angelfish eggs with some protection. Note the shade of blue as an indication of the concentration.*

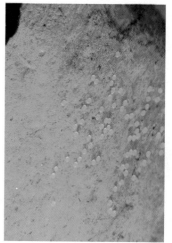

and steps have to be taken to ensure that the eggs are protected from the unwanted attentions of the parent fishes. However, certain cichlids that normally carry out quite dedicated brood care may repeatedly eat batches of eggs. This is often the case with inexperienced parent fishes, and once they have spawned two or three times, they eventually rear their young successfully. If, however, the egg eating extends beyond the first two or three batches of eggs – and assuming conditions in the tank are otherwise ideal – remove the newly hatched eggs from the parent fishes together with the rock or leaf on to which they were laid and hatch them in a separate tank. A gentle stream of air bubbles from an air stone will aid the passage of fresh water over the eggs. Treat any eggs that show signs of fungus promptly with a reliable remedy.

Below: Diagnosing and treating fish diseases becomes easier as your fishkeeping experience increases. Follow these guidelines, but always ask for veterinary help if needed.

Meeting the challenge

The fishkeeper may be faced with a variety of problems from time to time, many of which can be prevented by providing the fishes with the conditions they require, and then maintaining these conditions through proper tank care. There is, however, still a great deal we do not know about fish in general, and fish breeding in particular, which is one of the reasons why fishkeeping is the fascinating hobby that it is.

After all, what other hobby permits the keeping of beautifully marked living creatures from exotic places, such as the Amazon, Africa and the Far East, and allows their observation, breeding and growth from tiny juveniles to mature adults, all without leaving the confines of the living room? Fishkeeping really is a hobby – and a challenge – for everyone throughout the world.

Right: This table summarizes the symptoms and treatment of some common diseases of aquarium fish. Prompt diagnosis and effective treatment are the key to success.

General recommendations when treating fishes for disease

★ It is usually safer and easier to use a reliable proprietary brand of remedy with a proven track record and that has been developed against a background of scientific research.

★ Calculate the volume of any tanks or ponds carefully. Multiplying the tank length × width × water depth in cm and dividing by 1000 will give the volume in litres. Deduct 10 per cent from this for gravel and furnishings.

★ Turn off filtration through activated carbon during treatment since this will absorb remedies; ensure adequate aeration.

★ Do not overcrowd fishes during treatment; do not treat fishes in galvanized containers as poisoning may occur.

★ When treating delicate or expensive species, always try a remedy out on one or two before risking the whole batch.

★ Excessive amount of organic matter present in the tank will reduce the activity of most remedies.

★ Never mix remedies unless you know it is safe. A 50-75 percent water change or filtration through activated carbon for 12-24 hours should remove most of the active ingredients.

Recognizing and tackling fish diseases

Symptoms	Cause	Action
Off-white, grey or brown patches of 'cotton wool' on skin and fins	Fish fungus (e.g. *Saprolegnia*)	Add proprietary brand of fungal treatment to tank. Improve tank hygiene
White or grey filamentous patches around mouth, especially in livebearers	'Mouth fungus' (caused by a bacterium *Flexibacter*)	Isolate fish and treat with a proprietary remedy or with antibiotics from a veterinarian. Check tank care
White 'sugar or salt grains' on the skin and fins; scratching against rocks	White spot parasite (*Ichthyophthirius*)	Add proprietary brand of a white spot treatment to the affected tank. Quarantine and treat new fishes. Avoid certain live foods
Eroded edges to fins, split fins, reddening at fin base	Localized bacterial infection causing fin rot	Isolate fish and treat with an antibacterial remedy or with antibiotics from a veterinarian. Check tank care and hygiene
Reddening at fin base and vent, ulcers, open sores, etc	More systemic bacterial infection	Isolate fish and treat with antibiotics from a veterinarian. Check tank care
Grey, opaque film to skin, some reddening to flanks, laboured 'breathing', scratching against rocks	Various skin and gill parasites causing sliminess of the skin	Add proprietary white spot treatment or general anti-parasite treatment to tank. Quarantine and treat new fishes; check tank care
Pale 'holes' in head or flanks (especially along lateral line). Often affects Discus, other cichlids and gouramis	'Hole-in-the-head disease' caused by *Hexamita*	Isolate and treat with anti-parasite treatment or drugs from a veterinarian. Check tank care; improve hygiene
Loss of colour in Neons, emaciated appearance, often severe losses. May also affect other tetras, barbs and danios	Neon Tetra disease caused by the protozoan *Pleistophora*. Possibility of *Mycobacterium* infection (Fish TB)	No treatment possible. Isolate and destroy affected fishes; clean and refurbish tank; stock with fish from alternative source

Species section

The following pages provide detailed information on the care and breeding of a wide variety of popular aquarium fishes. Some of these, such as the livebearers, will often breed without any assistance, while others require careful conditioning, the correct water chemistry and patient vigilance from the hobbyist.

Fishkeepers with little or no experience of fish breeding should read through the introductory chapters of the book for basic information on tank requirements, feeding, water quality and disease problems. Many fishes have quite precise requirements in terms of pH (level of acidity or alkalinity), water hardness and temperature, and the needs of the species dealt with here are summarized in tables at the end of each section. Specially commissioned photographs show the types of tank set-ups required, with an emphasis on the practicalities of fish breeding rather than on the aesthetics of the breeding tank.

Having gained an appreciation of the various aspects of fish breeding, aquarists should select a hardy, easy-to-breed species for their first endeavours. As time goes by, and experience is gained, other more demanding species can be kept and bred. We must point out that the information provided in this section represents just one approach to the breeding of the selected species. Many can be bred successfully using other methods, and hobbyists are encouraged to experiment in their approach to fish breeding and to develop their own methods further. Whatever fishkeeping or fish breeding problems occur, there is always more than one solution, and thus plenty for all aquarists to discover.

Fishkeepers who have become fish breeders (and the transition is not that difficult) should share their knowledge with other enthusiasts by joining their local fish club, thus contributing to the further development of this fascinating hobby.

Introducing the cichlids

The cichlids are a large and very successful family of fishes that live in fresh and brackish waters in South and Central America and Africa, with a small number of species extending into southern Asia and North America. They are closely related to the sunfishes and perches of temperate regions. There are about 700 species of cichlids, of which as many as 500 species may live in the Rift Valley Lakes of East Africa.

The cichlids exhibit a number of extremely interesting behavioural traits, and for this reason they have long been popular with scientists, as well as aquarists. Notable is the degree of brood protection that the parent fish afford their fry. The cichlids can be divided into 'open spawners' and 'secretive spawners'.

Open spawners lay their eggs in an exposed position, such as on a flat stone or the surface of a leaf. The parent fishes are often similar in form and coloration, and both may guard the eggs, fry and surrounding territory. Dwarf cichlids, such as the Ram (*Papiliochromis ramirezi*) and fish within the *Aequidens* genus, are examples of open spawners, as is the Firemouth Cichlid (*Cichlasoma meeki*), the Angelfish and Discus fishes (*Symphysodon* sp.).

Generally speaking, secretive spawners lay their eggs in a small cave or similar site. The parent fishes are usually easily distinguished, with the male being larger and more brightly coloured, and with the female usually taking a more active part in the care of the eggs and fry than her mate. The Krib (*Pelvicachromis pulcher*), and the *Apistogramma* dwarf cichlids, are examples of secretive spawners.

'Mouthbrooding', in which the female cares for the fertilized eggs by carrying them in her mouth until they hatch, is a specialized form of secretive spawning.

Right: *It is said that Angelfishes can sometimes be sexed by the more rounded breeding tube at the vent of the female, as shown here. As with Discus fishes, however, it is often necessary to buy a group of juveniles and let them pair off naturally.*

Angelfish

There are a number of species of freshwater angelfish, although it is *Pterophyllum scalare* which is the most frequently kept and bred in aquariums.

The Angelfish is a beautiful, graceful cichlid from northern South America, where it lives in overgrown, weedy, still or sluggishly flowing waters. It is now one of the most popular of all the cichlids among fishkeepers, and is available in a number of tank-bred forms.

Angelfish are one of the longer-lived aquarium fish; they may live for up to ten years or more under favourable conditions, compared to five or six years for many other commonly kept fish. The maximum length reached by this tall, disc-like fish with trailing fins is about 15cm (6in), although young fish 2-3cm (0.8-1.2in) long are commonly available from aquatic dealers.

Unfortunately, there are no reliable external sexual characteristics. Experienced fishkeepers, however, learn to recognize visible differences in breeding tube shape and size between male and female Angelfishes after watching spawning activity. This method of sexing is reasonably reliable but is only possible when the fish have already selected their own partners and are displaying breeding and courtship behaviour in the aquarium.

Above: *This is the original wild form of the Angelfish, the so-called Common Silver Angelfish, typically marked with four vertical stripes.*

Below: *One of the tank-bred forms of Angelfish developed throughout the world. Some of these artificial strains may prove a little delicate.*

Generally speaking, Angelfish are best suited to spacious, well-planted tanks, where they will gracefully glide through thickets of Amazon Swordplants (*Echinodorus* sp.) or *Vallisneria* sp. They are fine for a community tank, although large Angelfishes are somewhat partial to small tetras, and some barbs may nip their trailing fins. They are unlikely to breed successfully in a community tank, however.

A temperature of 25°C (77°F) will suit Angelfish, but avoid very hard, alkaline water. It is possible to keep and breed Angels on a diet of good quality flaked and freeze-dried foods, plus an occasional feed of a safe live food (see page 29).

Since there are no reliable external sexual characteristics, one approach is to buy about half a dozen 3-5cm (1.2-2in) fish – aged about two months – and let them pair off naturally. They should begin to pair off after a few weeks, and certainly no longer than a year. Alternatively, some dealers offer matched pairs of mature Angelfish, although their price can be quite high. Once a pair has been identified, transfer the fishes to a separate breeding tank previously set up along the following lines.

Although Angels will breed in smaller tanks, it is best to use one at least 60cm (24in) long and 38cm (15in) deep for each pair of adult fish. This tank should be fairly spartan in its decor: a covering of fine, well-washed gravel, a large Amazon Swordplant in a pot and a good-sized piece of slate or a flat rock leant against one end of the glass are the ideal furnishings. For breeding purposes, raise the water temperature to a steady 26-28°C (79-82°F) using a reliable heater-thermostat, and keep the water continuously filtered with a foam filter.

Following many years of 'domestication', Angelfish will now breed in water with a range of pH and

hardness values – so long as the water quality in a given tank does not fluctuate with time, and so long as very hard, alkaline water is avoided. Try to use water below 10° dH (general hardness) and with a pH value below 7. Tapwater, so long as it is not too hard or alkaline, is fine. Be sure to treat it with a good tapwater conditioner before using it in the aquarium, however. Furthermore, most egglayers benefit from the regular use of a blackwater tonic, available from pet and aquatic stores.

Once established in their breeding tank, the Angels will eventually spawn on the leaves of the Amazon Swordplant or on the piece of slate, after meticulously cleaning their chosen site. This characteristic cleaning activity is usually a sure sign that spawning is about to start. Up to 400 eggs may be laid, and these are immediately fertilized by the male fish.

Right: *A pair of Angelfishes cleaning their spawning site, the leaves of an Amazon Swordplant, before egg-laying begins. Careful choice and cleaning of the spawning site plus meticulous brood care are features of many cichlid species bred in aquaria.*

Right: *A breeding set-up suitable for Angelfishes. The fishes will usually choose a flat area as a spawning site, although rather than using a piece of slate or Amazon Swordplant leaf, some individuals will spawn on the glass or even on filter tubes.*

Above: *This is the first in a sequence of photographs that show the breeding behaviour of Angelfishes. Here, the female fish assiduously cleans the chosen spawning site.*

Above: *The female lays a batch of eggs on the surface of a leaf as the male fish waits nearby ready to fertilize them. Up to 400 eggs may be deposited on the spawning site.*

Below: *Once each batch of eggs is laid, the male fish swims close to the spawning site to release the milt (sperm) that will fertilize them. This process is repeated many times.*

Below: *Once the eggs are laid and fertilized, parental concern (typical of the cichlids) begins in earnest. Here, the male inspects the eggs as the female hovers below him.*

Opinions seem to vary on the best way to care for the eggs and for the fry that subsequently hatch. Angelfish can make excellent parents, with the male *and* female fanning the eggs and caring for the brood. It is indeed a fascinating sight to watch the male and female fish fanning the eggs, delicately chewing them to clean them and release the fry, and then transporting the hatchlings to new, pre-cleaned sites at periodic intervals (every other day perhaps) around the aquarium. These may be leaf blades or inclined rock surfaces, or even shallow depressions dug in the gravel on the tank floor. Often the tiny fish are gathered together in a tight shoal every evening, and guarded by their parents during the night.

However, from time to time, fishkeepers come across pairs that eat batch after batch of eggs or fry. Ideally, give a pair of Angels two or three spawnings to prove themselves as parents. While this is going on, check the water quality in the breeding tank (i.e. for pH, hardness and nitrite or ammonia levels), ensure that the fish are offered a good, varied diet and be careful to avoid

Below: *Two or three days after being laid and fertilized, the eggs hatch into tiny fry. The young fishes feed on their yolk sacs for several days before they require feeding by the fishkeeper.*

unnecessary disturbances once the eggs have been laid.

If the fish, even when given 'ideal' conditions, continue to eat each brood they produce, you will need to remove the subsequent batches as soon as they are laid. Transfer the eggs, along with the leaf or piece of slate to which they are attached, swiftly and carefully to a jar or small aquarium containing 5-10 litres (1-2.2 gallons) of water from the breeding tank. If the eggs are laid on a leaf, weight this down in the hatching tank to prevent it floating on the water surface. Heat the water to 26-28°C (79-82°F) and gently aerate it to ensure a passage of water over the eggs, which will hatch after a period of two or three days.

Egg fungus can be a problem, especially if the eggs are reared away from the parents. Thus, it is a good idea to treat the hatching tank with the recommended dose of fungus treatment for eggs before any signs of fungus become evident.

After hatching, the young fry will continue to feed on the yolk sac for a further three or four days. As soon as the fry become free swimming and are feeding on liquid fry food and newly hatched brineshrimp, transfer them to a larger aquarium of about 50 litres (11 gallons), and provide gentle filtration and regular partial water changes of 25 percent a week.

After feeding eagerly on newly hatched brineshrimp, the free-swimming Angelfish fry will soon accept powdered baby fish foods, finely ground flake and, eventually, the same food as their parents. During the first few weeks, offer them food as often as five or six times a day, cutting this down to three or four feeds as the fish grow. Avoid overfeeding and tank pollution by carefully gauging each meal to the size of their appetite.

Correctly cared for, the fish will grow rapidly. However, to keep conditions in the rearing tank satisfactory, some thinning out of the stock will be necessary. Local aquarium dealers may take your surplus stock, and fish clubs often organize auctions, raffles or fish exchanges to solve your dilemma.

Discus

In common with Angelfish, Discus fishes (*Symphysodon* sp.) come from the slow-moving, weedy waters of northern South America. There are, in fact, two species of Discus, one of which is further divided into three subspecies. Therefore, we have:

1 *Symphysodon discus*, Heckel's Discus

2 *Symphysodon aequifasciata*:

   a) *S. aequifasciata aequifasciata*, Green Discus

   b) *S.aequifasciata haraldi*, Blue Discus

   c) *S.aequifasciata axelrodi*, Brown Discus

Furthermore, a number of tank-produced strains and crosses are now available, although it is the Brown Discus that is most widely kept and bred by aquarists.

The Brown Discus may grow to 12 to 15cm (4.7-6in) in length, and in the aquarium it requires somewhat similar conditions to the Angelfish. However, Discus are generally more fussy with regard to water conditions and diet. Most Discus prefer soft, slightly acid water (general hardness less than 5°dH, carbonate hardness less that 3°dH, pH 5.5-6.5), that is well filtered and aerated, and kept within the temperature range 28-32°C (82-90°F). Regular partial water changes and the frequent use of a blackwater tonic are also important, as is scrupulous tank hygiene. To maintain the high degree of cleanliness necessary in the Discus tank, do not provide gravel on the aquarium floor and limit the decoration to one or two smooth-edged, flat stones and one or two potted Amazon Swords or similar broad-Leaved plants.

The Discus is *not* a fish for the community tank, although a shoal of *Corydoras* catfishes or a shoal of Neons or Cardinal Tetras are ideal companions for this delicate, peaceful cichlid when it is kept in a spacious display tank.

Most Discus fish will accept scraped lean, raw meat (especially ox heart), *Tubifex*, *Daphnia* and whiteworms, although a more satisfactory diet would consist of a good-quality flaked food, with only occasional feeds of the above and/or freeze-dried foods. Variety in the diet is important to Discus, although you should take particular care to avoid overfeeding and be sure to remove any uneaten food immediately with a siphon tube or dip tube.

Since, like Angelfish, there are no reliable external sexual characteristics, preparing for Discus breeding is similar to that described for Angels. Obtain a shoal of five or six juveniles, and eventually a pair should separate off from the rest. Discus mature at about 12 months of age, and each fish displays to its would-be partner by various delicate swimming manoeuvres, including fin opening and closing.

As spawning time approaches, the pair will select a spawning site – often the vertical side of an earthenware pot or the leaf of an Amazon Swordplant – and spend some time delicately cleaning it. Since young Discus sometimes do not split off from the shoal until spawning is imminent, isolating the prospective parents may be difficult. However, once a pair has been identified, and perhaps spawned successfully, they may then be maintained in their own breeding tank. Otherwise, as the pair separate off from the shoal for the first time, it may be a good idea to remove the remaining shoal members to leave the prospective parents in comparative peace.

The laying and fertilization of the pale brown, oval eggs may take an hour or more, and these hatch after 48 hours, but they do not leave the egg shells for a further 12-18 hours. During this time, the parents religiously fan water over their brood with their pectoral fins. Batches of 150 eggs are about average, although a large mature pair may lay up to 400 eggs. Egg fungus is not usually a problem in Discus breeding, as the affected eggs seldom appear to infect nearby healthy, fertile eggs. (Egg fungus is discussed on page 35.)

Two or three days after spawning, the parent fish move the tiny fry from the spawning site to another 'safe spot' in the aquarium, often moving the fry several more times until they become free swimming, five to seven days after spawning.

By this time, the skin of the parent fishes has developed a slimy, mucus coating and it is on this that the free-swimming fry feed. For up to a week, the high-protein slime produced by the parents nourishes the fry, and the tiny fish can be seen nibbling at their parents' skin in the flank and head region. In fact, the parent fish are quite protective of their young, and readily shield them from any impending danger. Feeding a large brood of fry can impose quite a nutritional burden on the parent fishes, and so during this time provide

Below: *Brown Discus (*Symphysodon aequifasciata axelrodi*) at home in a suitably spartan aquarium. This is the most commonly available colour form of the Discus fishes.*

47

Right: *A tank set-up for keeping and breeding Discus fishes should be purposely sparse in its furnishings. A flat rock or piece of slate will form an ideal spawning surface on which about 150 eggs are usually laid.*

Far right: *An attentive Discus fish fans water over the cluster of eggs. It is not uncommon for the parents to eat the first two or three batches of eggs, but then they often settle down to rearing a 'family' successfully.*

Below right: *Young Discus fry feed on the nutritious slime produced on the parents' skin around the head and flanks. This feeding process may last for a week or so, during which time the parents need a wholesome and varied diet to sustain them.*

them with a nutritious and varied diet.

When the fry have been free swimming for about a week or so, offer them liquid fry food, newly hatched brineshrimp, liquidized ox heart and, eventually, finely powdered dry foods. Provide frequent small meals and avoid tank pollution from uneaten food.

With correct care and a good varied diet, Discus can reach 3cm (1.2in) in diameter just a few weeks after hatching, looking for all the world like miniature versions of their parents. At this stage, remove them from their parents and rear them on in a large, well-filtered aquarium. Be sure to carry out frequent partial water changes. As always, a good varied diet will continue to encourage them to grow rapidly. Eventually, you may need to cull or sell off a proportion of very large broods to enable the remainder to develop into fully grown, healthy fish.

As with many cichlids, a pair of Discus fishes may eat their first brood or two of eggs, but then often go on to become model parents. Compulsive egg eaters are perhaps best split up and paired with other fish. Details of the artificial rearing of Discus fry away from their parents have been recorded, but these are not provided here because the event is much less common and successful than it is with Angelfishes.

Firemouth Cichlid

The Firemouth Cichlid, *Cichlasoma meeki*, was first described in 1812 and is a member of a large genus of medium-sized, very popular cichlids found in South, Central and even parts of North America. The Firemouth is a native of Central America, where it often occurs in quiet backwaters, although the species has also been recorded from underground caves.

It may be thought of as being typically 'cichlid' in body shape, with the mature fish being anything from 8 to 15cm (3.2-6in) in length. Most tank specimens seldom grow beyond about 10 or 12cm (4-4.7in), though. The mature male fish is usually larger and noticeably more colourful than the female, with more pointed dorsal and anal fins.

The Firemouth will live in a community tank and is usually aggressive only to other members of the same species, and then only when breeding. Robust plants are best, as this fish can be a little hard on real plants at spawning time. A steady temperature around 24-25°C (75-77°F) is recommended, and this

fish is not fussy with regard to pH and hardness, although extreme values are best avoided. Feed Firemouths on good-quality flake foods, with occasional freeze-dried and safe live foods for variety.

It really is preferable to breed this cichlid in a special breeding tank. This should be about 60cm (24in) long, furnished with a layer of sandy gravel and a few rocks and roots, plus one or two robust or plastic plants. The water conditions can be as described above, with suitable filtration supplied by a foam filter. Naturally, a good varied diet and regular partial water changes are important to bring the fish into breeding condition.

The Firemouth spawns on stones or pieces of wood in the open. The meticulous cleaning of the chosen spawning site is usually a sign that spawning is imminent. Both parents guard the eggs and fry, the latter hatching out after about two or three days. Batches consisting of several hundred eggs are not uncommon. Feed the young free-swimming fry on liquid fry food, newly hatched brineshrimp and similar foods. They will soon grow and begin feeding on powdered dried foods and crumbled flake foods. Unlike some related *Cichlasoma* species, the Firemouth does not premasticate food for its young. Thus, be sure to give the fry regular small meals several times a day to keep them well nourished.

Left: *Although Firemouth Cichlids usually spawn on flat stones in the open, they will also make use of 'caves' provided by flowerpots positioned on their sides in the aquarium. Once spawning is over, both parents guard eggs and fry.*

Below: *A tank set-up suitable for breeding cichlids, such as the Firemouth. Since real plants may be uprooted by the fishes, use plastic plants instead or dispense with them altogether. The flattish stones will form ideal spawning sites.*

Once the fry are feeding well and begin to break away from their parents, move them to a growing-on tank. Since the brood size of Firemouths can be quite large, good filtration and regular partial water changes are again vital.

Many cichlids of modest size go about their daily aquarium business reasonably peacefully, but turn very territorially aggressive during breeding periods. However, there are other smaller, peaceful cichlids from the genus *Aequidens* that are not only suitable for community aquariums, but which also breed readily. These are all open spawners. They include the Flag Cichlid or Sheepshead Acara, (*A.curviceps*), and the fairly shy Keyhole Cichlid (*A.maroni*). The larger Blue Acara, (*A.pulcher*), although a very prolific spawner, is not to be trusted with smaller decorative fishes, such as Neon Tetras, which it eventually finds too tempting a meal to resist!

Right: *Yolk sac fry of the Blue Acara,* Aequidens pulcher, *cluster together soon after hatching. The young feed on the yolk for several days and need no extra food supplied to them.*

Far right: *Once the yolk sac is absorbed, the fry require feeding with newly hatched brineshrimp or a proprietary liquid fry food.*

Centre right: *The Keyhole Cichlid,* Aequidens maroni *– a relatively peaceful cichlid – is shown here cleaning its chosen spawning site.*

Bottom right: *A pair of Keyhole Cichlids spawning. The eggs hatch in a few days and both parents guard the fry. The young may remain with the parents for up to six months.*

Below: *A male Firemouth Cichlid guarding a shoal of young fry. Broods of several hundred young are not uncommon in this species.*

The Egyptian Mouthbrooder

Described to science in 1903, the Egyptian Mouthbrooder *Pseudocrenilabrus* (also known as *Hemihaplochromis* or *Haplochromis*) *multicolor*, comes from East Africa, especially the Nile region, where it lives in a variety of waters. It is quite an attractively marked fish, the males showing an iridescent sheen to their bodies and often, a red edge to their fins. The female is relatively sombre.

This fish may grow to a length of 8cm (3.2in) and is relatively peaceful, except at spawning time. It can be kept and even bred in the community tank. It is a hardy fish and perhaps an ideal cichlid for beginners. Provide a steady temperature in the range 22-25°C (72-77°F) and avoid extremes of hardness and pH. Since the male fish is somewhat territorial,

Below: A breeding tank for a pair of Egyptian Mouthbrooders. The male will often establish a territory around a flat rock or other spawning site. Be sure to provide sufficient rocks and similar furnishings that will allow the male to set up his territory.

ensure that the tank is reasonably well planted and includes some rocky caves and refuges. The Egyptian Mouthbrooder will thrive on a diet of high-quality flaked foods, with the occasional use of freeze-dried foods.

Although it will breed in a community tank, it is probably best to breed the Egyptian Mouthbrooder in a special breeding tank, set up along the lines described above. This tank need not necessarily be very large; 45x25x25cm (18x10x10in) is ideal.

Breeding should be relatively straightforward. The male fish first establishes a territory, often centred around a chosen flat rock or other suitable spawning site, and then courts the female. Eventually, he leads her to the spawning site, where, if mature, she will deposit her eggs. Over a period of about half an hour, the female lays up to 100 eggs in batches of a dozen or so, collecting each batch of eggs in her mouth. The male may quickly fertilize the eggs before the female has a chance to pick them up. Alternatively, as is the case with some of the other mouthbrooders, the female may

Above: *The Egyptian Mouthbrooder,* Pseudocrenilabrus multicolor. *The female is less brightly coloured than the male. Unlike some other cichlids, this species does not usually form a firm pair bond. The female takes care of the fry, leaving the male free to mate with other females.*

stimulate the male into releasing his milt into the water by nipping his anal fin, whereupon she draws the milt into her mouth and over the eggs she has collected, thereby fertilizing them.

Remove the male once spawning is completed; these fish do not seem to form a pair bond like some other cichlids, and one male may mate with a number of females.

Young, inexperienced fish may have difficulty in spawning successfully and rearing the first brood or two. However, with practice and (on the part of the aquarist) patience, they usually get it right.

The fertilized eggs remain in the throat sac of the female for up to 10 days, by which time they will have hatched, and the young fry will have absorbed their yolk sacs. As soon as the young fish begin to leave their mother's mouth, offer them liquid fry food and/or newly hatched brineshrimp several times a day. Soon they will graduate on to a diet of powdered dried foods, crumbled flakes and, eventually, the same food as their parents.

As the fry become more independent from the female – perhaps a week after first leaving the safety of her mouth – remove her from the tank before she confuses her brood with tasty food morsels. Allow the female to recover away from the attentions of the male for a few days. Feed her on a good varied diet during this period, since she may not have eaten for two or three weeks, i.e. since first spawning.

As the fry grow, pay particular attention to filtration and aeration, and increase the frequency of partial water changes. Filtration using a good-quality foam filter is particularly beneficial in the breeding tank, since such filters pose no threat to delicate fry – as do, for example, some high-turnover power filters – and yet provide effective filtration and valuable aeration at the same time.

Left: *A male Burton's Mouthbrooder, Astatotilapia burtoni, which may reach a length of 10cm (4in). Note the 'egg spots' on the anal fin, which play an important role in the mating sequence. The female nipping at these spots stimulates the male to release his milt for fertilization.*

Centre left: *A pair of Burton's Mouthbrooders spawning in the aquarium. The care and breeding of this species is similar to that described for the Egyptian Mouthbrooder, except that the water should be slightly warmer.*

Bottom left: *A female Burton's Mouthbrooder with young in her mouth. Mouthbrooding is an extreme form of brood care, and is also practised by certain other cichlids, such as some species of Lake Malawi cichlids, and also by certain gouramis. Whilst 'brooding', the female does not feed and her condition can deteriorate noticeably.*

Below: *At the first sign of danger, the young fry seek refuge in their mother's mouth. Try not to disturb a female mouthbrooder with eggs or fry, since too much disruption can cause her to eat them. The young fry remain close to the mother until they can swim away independently.*

Burton's Mouthbrooder

Burton's Mouthbrooder (*Astatotilapia (Haplochromis) burtoni*) originates from central and eastern Africa. It may grow to a length of 10cm (4in), with the female being slightly smaller. A somewhat quarrelsome fish, it is best kept in a single-species aquarium set up along similar lines to that already described for the Egyptian Mouthbrooder, but with a water temperature maintained at around 25-26°C (77-79°F).

The care and breeding of Burton's Mouthbrooder is, in fact, very similar to that previously described for *Pseudocrenilabrus multicolor*. However, the fish is mentioned here because, in common with many other mouthbrooding cichlids, the male has a small number of round 'egg spots' on his anal fin. It has been suggested that when the female is busy collecting the eggs and sees these spots on the nearby fin of the male fish, she is encouraged to nip at them, thereby stimulating the male to release the milt. Taken into the female's mouth, the milt passes over the eggs, fertilizing them in the process. Such 'egg spots' are missing from the anal fin of *Pseudocrenilabrus multicolor*, although the female of this species may nip at the pale edge of the male's anal fin and achieve the same result.

Dwarf cichlids

Although the cichlids are extremely popular among aquarists, many of the larger and commonly available species can be rather aggressive, particularly at spawning time, and also destructive towards tank decor, especially rooted plants. Therefore, they are generally unsuitable for the community tank and often have to be kept in relatively large, single-species aquariums.

However, the so-called 'dwarf cichlids' do not usually display the same undesirable behavioural traits as their larger relatives and are, in fact, ideal inmates for the planted mixed-species tank, where they will usually thrive and even breed.

The dwarf cichlids are linked by the fact that they rarely grow more than about 10cm (4in) long. The majority of these species originate from tropical and subtropical South America and include certain *Apistogramma* species, such as *Apistogramma agassizi*, (Agassizi's Dwarf Cichlid), *Papiliochromis ramirezi* (the Ram or Butterfly Dwarf Cichlid), as well as fish within the *Nannacara, Crenicara* and one or two other related genera.

A small number of dwarf cichlids also originate from West Africa, notably the Krib (*Pelvicachromis pulcher*). The smaller species of East African Rift Lake cichlids are not usually referred to as dwarf cichlids in aquarist circles, and the mouthbrooding breeding habits of the dwarf Egyptian mouthbrooder (*Pseudocrenilabrus multicolor*) have been dealt with on page 54.

No more than a dozen or so species of dwarf cichlids are commonly kept by aquarists. Here, we review the methods recommended for the successful spawning of a selection of these handsome and interesting species.

Krib or Rainbow Dwarf Cichlid

The Krib or Rainbow Dwarf Cichlid is currently known to scientists as *Pelvicachromis pulcher*, although it may be referred to in older literature as *Pelmatochromis kribensis*. It is an attractive and peaceful fish ideal for beginners, and commonly occurs in both fresh and slightly brackish waters in its West African home.

This species may reach 8 or 10cm (3.2-4in) in length, with the male being slightly longer and slimmer than the female. The mature female tends to be more brightly coloured than the male, with her red belly being particularly striking, although the male fish does have longer, more pointed fins. Further distinguishing features are that the male has dark spots in the upper part of the caudal fin, while the female has a dark spot on the rear part of the dorsal fin.

The Krib, a secretive spawner like most dwarf cichlids, thrives as a pair in a community tank containing plenty of hiding places in the form of caves, flowerpots, half-coconut shells, etc. They seem to prefer a steady temperature of 25°C (77°F), and good filtration and regular partial water changes are also important. The Krib appears fairly adaptable with regard to pH and water hardness, although extreme values should be avoided. Some aquarists prefer to add a little aquarium salt (1gm per 5 litres/about one teaspoonful per gallon) to a Krib

Above: *The Krib,* Pelvicachromis pulcher, *usually lays its eggs on the roof of a cave. Both parents then accept the responsibility of guarding the eggs and young fry until they are able to fend for themselves.*

Below: *In this set-up a flowerpot makes an ideal spawning 'cave' for the Krib. This fish will usually breed at around 25°C (77°F), although raising the temperature two or three degrees can have a stimulating effect.*

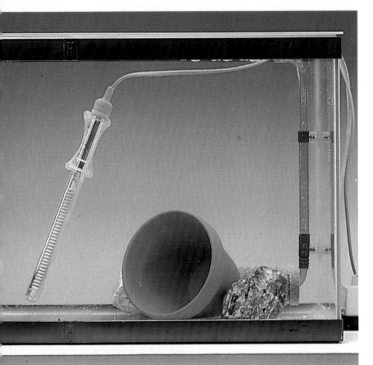

Above: *Borelli's Dwarf Cichlid,* Apistogramma borelli, *is another easy-to-breed fish. The males can be quite territorial, which may lead to frequent confrontations, such as this head-on encounter, if more than one male is kept in a small tank.*

Right: *Laying eggs on the roof of a cave necessitates some impressive underwater acrobatics by this male and female Borelli's Dwarf Cichlid.*

aquarium, although it is possible to keep and breed them in quite soft water. This fish can be maintained on a diet of good-quality prepared foods, along with occasional feeds of a safe live food (see page 29).

Breeding is best attempted in an aquarium approximately 50cm (20in) long, set up along the lines indicated above. Since the Krib becomes particularly territorial at spawning time, exclude all other fish species from the tank. Having said that, the Krib will breed in a community tank, in which case the rest of the tank inmates will find themselves confined to one half of the aquarium by the parent fishes. In fact, if the aquarium is large enough – say 100cm (39in) long – with plenty of caves and hiding places, several pairs of Kribs can be kept in the same tank.

A mature pair of Kribs – the female distinguished by her bright coloration and rounded belly – will select a suitable cave for spawning, and the female will lay up to 100 or more yellow-brown eggs on to the roof of the cave. Both parents usually guard these eggs, which hatch after three or four days. The fry become free swimming within a week and then you can offer them regular, small meals of newly hatched brineshrimp, liquid fry food and finely powdered dried foods. If you wish, you can siphon the brineshrimp directly into the tank using a piece of air line, directing the cloud of tiny crustaceans towards the shoal of Krib fry.

The parent fish will protect their fry during the first few weeks, keeping them in a tightly packed shoal. Eventually, however, the fry will become noticeably more independent of their parents and this is the time to separate them into another tank for rearing on. A varied diet, good filtration and regular, partial water changes will encourage them to grow rapidly.

Other species of dwarf cichlids that spawn in caves and that you can breed in a fashion similar to that described for the Krib include Agassizi's Dwarf Cichlid (*Apistogramma agassizi*) and Borelli's Dwarf Cichlid (*A. borelli*). Both these species come from South America and appear to prefer water that is neutral to slightly acid and of only moderate hardness (pH 6.5, general hardness less than 8-10°dH). A slightly higher temperature (around 26-27°C/79-81°F), and a little floating vegetation in the aquarium are also recommended when attempting to breed these fish. Although the parent fish may, as with many cichlids, eat their first brood of eggs, they invariably go on to breed successfully. Since the female of these two species takes care of the eggs and young fry, and actively drives other fish from their vicinity, it is best to remove the male *Apistogramma* immediately after spawning, although it is possible to keep and breed these fish in a tank containing a single male and a 'harem' of several females.

Below: *A pair of Kribs with a shoal of fry. Brood care is advanced in many cichlids, and the Krib is no exception. Broods of up to 100 or more are not* uncommon, with the eggs taking between three and four days to hatch. Feed the young fry on newly hatched brineshrimp.

Ram or Butterfly Dwarf Cichlid

The Ram or Butterfly Dwarf Cichlid has a somewhat complicated taxonomic history. Although not discovered until 1947, it has been known by a number of scientific names, including *Apistogramma ramirezi* and also *Microgeophagus ramirezi* (the latter being still favoured by some authorities). However, it is now generally accepted that the scientific name of the Ram should be *Papiliochromis ramirezi*.

This fish comes from northwestern South America, although very little is known about its habits in the wild. Mature fish, which may measure 5 or 6cm (2-2.4in) in length, are often very colourful indeed, although their coloration may depend on whether they are wild-caught or tank-bred specimens. It is said that Rams bred on tropical fish farms are fed on hormones or special diets to make them appear more colourful than they otherwise would be.

Above: *The Ram,* Papiliochromis ramirezi, *is a popular if rather delicate dwarf cichlid. It is an 'open spawner', laying its eggs on a flat stone or in a depression in the aquarium gravel.*

Sexing the Ram is relatively easy, since the females are generally smaller than the males, with a shorter dorsal fin and, at spawning time, a red belly. The male often has a longer second or third ray in the dorsal fin.

This dwarf cichlid is a rather shy, delicate fish. It can be kept in a community tank, where it will patrol the lower reaches, although the tank should not contain any very active or aggressive species. Soft, slightly acid to neutral water (general hardness less than 3 or 4°dH, pH 6.5-7.0) at a temperature around 25°C (77°F) seems preferred, and is quite important for successful breeding. The Ram will thrive on a diet of prepared foods, with the occasional use of a safe live food.

In a well-planted, 60-100cm (24-39in) aquarium containing some cave or bogwood hiding places and some flat stones, a small group of, say, two or three males and four or five females should spawn successfully. The fish will separate off into pairs and the prospective parents will begin cleaning and defending a chosen spawning site. This may be a flat stone or a shallow depression dug in the aquarium gravel.

When the time is right, the female lays 100-200 eggs and these, along with the fry that hatch after two or three days, are vigorously guarded by the parents. When the fry become free swimming after a further two or three days, feed them on liquid fry food, newly hatched brineshrimp and, eventually, finely powdered dry foods and then the same foods as their parents.

Some aquarists have experienced problems with parents eating successive broods of eggs. If this occurs, remove the flat stone complete with the eggs to a 10-15 litre (2.2-3.3 gallon) aquarium containing the same water as the breeding tank, and rear the young fish separately from their parents.

Other species of dwarf cichlids that are open spawners and lay their eggs in the open on a previously cleaned flat surface include the Checkerboard Cichlid (*Crenicara filamentosa*) and the Golden-eyed Dwarf Cichlid (*Nannacara anomala*). The latter species will also spawn in a cave or similar situation, with the female later moving her young to a pit in the aquarium gravel. All of these fish are probably less fussy than the Ram as far as pH and water hardness are concerned. On occasion, it may be safer to remove the male fish after spawning is completed. Fry rearing in these fishes is similar to that described for the Ram.

In conclusion, the dwarf cichlids are generally peaceful fishes that, given the correct spawning sites, will allow even relatively novice fishkeepers to observe some of the fascinating aspects of brood care for which the cichlid family are so famous. And all without setting up a large, single-species aquarium.

Below: *The Golden-eyed Dwarf Cichlid,* Nannacara anomala, *may spawn in a cave and then the female moves the fry to a pit in the gravel.*

BREEDING TABLE – CICHLIDS

FISH SPECIES	SEXUAL CHARACTERISTICS	WATER CONDITIONS FOR BREEDING
Angelfish *(Pterophyllum scalare)*	No reliable external sexual characteristics	26-28°C (79-82°F); pH less than 7.0; hardness less than 10°dH
Discus *(Symphysodon aequifasciata)*	No reliable external sexual characteristics	28-32°C (82-90°F); pH 5.5-6.5; hardness less than 5°dH
Firemouth Cichlid *(Cichlasoma meeki)*	Male larger, with longer fins and more colourful than female	25°C (77°F); avoid extremes of pH and hardness
Egyptian Mouthbrooder *(Pseudocrenilabrus multicolor)*	Male more brightly coloured than female	22-25°C (72-72°F); avoid extremes of pH and hardness

DWARF CICHLIDS

FISH SPECIES	SEXUAL CHARACTERISTICS	WATER CONDITIONS FOR BREEDING
Ram *(Papiliochromis ramirezi)*	Male larger, with more flowing fins	22-25°C (72-77°F); avoid extremes of pH and hardness
Krib *(Pelvicachromis pulcher)*	Male longer, slimmer, with more pointed fins. Mature female has a noticeably red belly	25-28°C (77-82°F); avoid extremes of pH and hardness

SPAWNING METHOD AND BROOD CARE	NUMBER OF EGGS AND HATCHING TIME	FIRST FOOD FOR FRY
Eggs laid on flat upright surface; brood cared for by both parents	Up to 1000 eggs, usually several hundred; 48-72 hours to hatch	Liquid fry food; newly hatched brineshrimp
Eggs laid on flat upright surface; brood cared for by both parents; young may feed on skin slime of parent fishes	Up to 400 eggs, usually around 150; 48-60 hours to hatch	Liquid fry food; newly hatched brineshrimp
Eggs laid on flat stone or piece of wood; eggs and fry guarded by both parents	Several hundred eggs; 48-72 hours to hatch	Liquid fry food; newly hatched brineshrimp; finely powdered dried foods
Eggs and fry 'brooded' in mouth of female	100 or so eggs; young fry leave mother's mouth after 10 days	Newly hatched brineshrimp; finely powdered dried foods
Eggs laid on flat stone; guarded by both parents	100-200 eggs; 48-72 hours to hatch	Liquid fry food; newly hatched brineshrimp
Eggs laid on roof of cave; eggs and fry protected by both parents	100 or more; 72-96 hours to hatch	Liquid fry food; newly hatched brineshrimp

Gouramis and their relatives

The so-called labyrinth or anabantoid fishes consist of four families and about 70 species of freshwater fishes from tropical Africa and Southeast Asia. Characteristic of the anabantoids is an accessory respiratory organ, the labyrinth, which is an extension of the gill chamber and is situated behind the eyes/gills region of the head. Richly supplied with blood vessels, it allows these fishes to 'breathe' atmospheric air when oxygen levels in the water are low. This can be an important survival adaptation in the warm, stagnant waters in which they naturally occur.

Most of the commonly kept aquarium species are relatively undemanding and, given a certain amount of special attention, will breed in suitably set-up tanks. Many of the anabantoids are 'bubble-nesters', and incubate their eggs in floating 'nests' specially constructed by the male fish. Many species, such as the Dwarf Gourami (*Colisa lalia*), Banded Gourami (*C. fasciata*), Pearl Gourami (*Trichogaster leeri*), Siamese Fighting Fish (*Betta splendens*), and the Paradisefish (*Macropodus opercularis*), build quite substantial nests, and even incorporate plant fragments. Other species, including the Honey Gourami (*Colisa chuna*) and Kissing Gourami (*Helostoma temmincki*), make little or no attempts at nest building. In addition, the Chocolate Gourami (*Sphaerichthys osphromenoides*) and a number of fighting fish (*Betta* spp.) are mouthbrooders.

Gouramis

Most of the commonly kept gouramis are bubble-nesters and can be bred in a fashion similar to that described below for the dwarf gourami.

The Dwarf Gourami (*Colisa lalia*) comes from eastern India, where it lives in still, heavily weeded waters. It may reach a length of 5cm (2in), and the female fish is less brightly coloured and has more rounded dorsal and anal fins than the male.

For breeding purposes, it is best to keep the male and female fish separate for a few weeks and bring them into condition on a diet of high-quality flaked and freeze-dried foods, with occasional feeds of safe live foods. As the female becomes grossly distended with eggs, transfer her to a 45-60cm (18-24in) breeding

Below: Use warm, fairly shallow water with only very gentle aeration to breed anabantoid bubble-nesters. Warm, humid air above the water is important for the development of the labyrinth organ in the fry.

Above: *The Dwarf Gourami,* Colisa lalia, *is a popular aquarium species. The mature male is more colourful than the more rounded mature female. The Dwarf Gourami is now available in various tank-bred forms.*

tank containing about 12 or 15cm (4.7-6in) of water heated to a steady 28-30°C (82-86°F). Ideally, use neutral water with a general hardness of less than 7-8°dH. The tank should contain plenty of fine-leaved plants, such as *Cabomba* or *Myriophyllum*, to act as a refuge for the female, and some floating plants – *Riccia*, for example – fragments of which the male can use in constructing his bubble-nest. Fit a transparent plastic cover or a cover glass on the tank to keep the humidity and temperature high and help to maintain the bubble-nest in good condition.

One or two days after introducing the female into the breeding tank, release the male fish with her. His coloration should heighten within a few minutes and, all being well, he should soon begin building a bubble-nest. This he does by taking in a large gulp of air at the water surface and converting it into many smaller bubbles that are passed into the gill chamber and coated with an 'anti-burst' agent before release.

During and immediately after building the bubble-nest, the male fish displays to the female, which usually ends with both fish embracing near the nest and a burst of twenty or so eggs being released. These fall to the tank floor but are then collected up by the male and spat into the bubble-nest. Over a couple of hours, several hundred eggs are laid. Remove the female once spawning is completed, taking care not to disturb the delicate structure of the nest.

Since eager male gouramis – and the males of many other anabantoids – can sometimes be a little rough with immature or unwilling females, be sure to condition the parent fishes first and use only *mature* females in a well-planted tank. Try to ensure that the female goes into the breeding tank in advance of the male so that he has to court her in *her* territory. Otherwise, if she is introduced to him, he may well attack her as an intruder, despite her well-conditioned appearance.

Within the bubble-nest, the eggs hatch after about 24 hours and the fry become free swimming after a further three or four days. To be on the safe side, it is probably a good idea to

Above: *A spawning sequence of the Dwarf Gourami. First, the male builds a bubble-nest from bubbles he 'blows' at the water surface, mixing some plant fragments into it.*

Below: *The spawning sequence begins once the male has persuaded the female to join him below the bubble-nest. His bright colour and breeding display attract the female.*

remove the male fish once the eggs have hatched, since leaving him in any longer than this may result in him eating some of the fry, although this behaviour does vary from fish to fish.

Feed the free-swimming fry on liquid fry food and very small live food, such as green water (algae in suspension) and infusorians, graduating on to newly hatched brineshrimp after a week or so. Offer several small feeds each day, taking care to avoid tank pollution. After a week or 10 days, install a foam filter and begin to make regular partial water changes. Be sure to refill the tank with water which is at the correct temperature and which has been treated with a reliable conditioner to eliminate chlorine.

Above: *Spawning then follows as the pair embrace below the bubble-nest. The eggs are laid in bursts and gathered into the nest by the male. Several hundred eggs may be laid.*

Below: *The Pearl Gourami,* Trichogaster leeri, *can be bred in a fashion similar to the Dwarf Gourami. Sometimes the pair fall to the tank floor during their spawning embrace. The bubble-nest is a form of brood protection, ensuring that the eggs and young fry are kept in the upper, oxygen-rich layers of the water. Over-vigorous aeration and turbulence will destroy a bubble-nest.*

During this time, it is vital to keep the water shallow – less than 15cm (6in) deep – and to keep the tank covered; at about two to four weeks of age, the labyrinth organ will begin to develop and any chilling of the air just above the water surface can have disastrous effects on the tiny fry. Similarly, in order for the labyrinth to develop properly, the fry must have easy access to the water surface. Providing very gentle aeration will prevent the formation of an oily film on the water surface that might otherwise interfere with the proper development of the labyrinth organ.

At about four to six weeks of age the fry should be feeding on crumbled flake foods and similar foods. About five or six weeks after hatching, the labyrinth should be formed and the tank can be topped up to full depth.

Many gourami fry are cannibalistic as they grow, so be sure to grade the brood frequently and remove the larger fish to avoid losses.

While most gouramis are bubble-nesters, at least one species – the Chocolate Gourami – is a mouthbrooder (see also pages 54-57).

Above: *The Chocolate Gourami,* Sphaerichthys osphromenoides, *is a delicate species that mouthbroods a batch of up to 80 eggs and fry.*

Chocolate Gourami

The Chocolate Gourami was first described to science in 1860 under the name *Osphromenus malayanus,* although current scientific thinking tells us that it should be known as *Sphaerichthys osphromenoides.*

The Chocolate Gourami is a close relative of the Dwarf Gourami (*Colisa lalia*). It comes from Sumatra and Malaya, and may reach 5 or 6cm (2-2.4in) in length. It is not an easy fish to sex, although mature females tend to be smaller than males and more rounded in overall shape. The male fish also has a light edge to its fins.

Below: *The Banded Gourami,* Colisa fasciata, *in a spawning embrace near the bubble-nest. The eggs can be seen emerging from the female fish. They will hatch in the layer of bubbles.*

It is quite a delicate species and does need rather special care in the aquarium. A 100 litre (22 gallon) tank will be suitable for eight to ten Chocolate Gouramis. Provide soft, slightly acid water (with a general hardness of less than 5°dH, pH6-6.5) at a temperature of about 25-30°C (77-86°F). It is probably best to keep this fish in a well-planted 'species' tank (i.e. restricted to one species only) where it can feed and be observed without interference from other, more robust fishes. Regular, partial water changes, efficient but gentle filtration (using foam filters, for example) and regular use of a blackwater tonic are all recommended. This fish will usually accept live food readily, although with patience it may be possible to persuade it to accept dried foods.

The Chocolate Gourami is not an easy fish to breed, and this is reflected by the fact that only relatively recently was it described as a mouthbrooder. At one time, some people even suspected it to be a livebearer!

Following a brief display, up to 80 eggs are produced and fertilized. The female then collects the eggs into her well-developed throat pouch and broods them inside for about three weeks. Inexperienced adult fishes may eat the first brood or two, but, as with many other fishes, they soon seem to realize what is required of them. About three weeks after spawning, the fully formed fry – 6-7mm (0.2-0.3in) long – leave the female's mouth.

In order to avoid the fry being eaten by other fish in the tank, remove the brooding female to a small rearing tank, perhaps of 10 litre (2.2 gallon) capacity, containing the same water as the set-up tank and some floating feathery leaved plants. After she has released her young, transfer her back into the set-up tank.

In the small rearing tank, the young fry will initially hang motionless among the plants and can be fed on liquid fry food or newly hatched brineshrimp. With regular but small feeds, regular partial water changes and an occasional check on aquarium pH, the fry appear to grow quite rapidly and may reach 14mm (0.55in) at five or six weeks of age. At this stage they look like perfectly formed miniature versions of their parents.

Correct and stable water conditions, in a clean, well-filtered tank seem important for maintaining and breeding this fish successfully.

Below: *A breeding tank for the Chocolate Gourami should contain soft, acid water at 25-30°C (77-86°F), with gentle filtration. Ideally, treat the water with a blackwater tonic.*

Above: *Male and female Fighting Fishes,* Betta splendens, *should be separated by a tank divider, and the divider removed once the male* begins nest building. If the female is not receptive to the advances of the male, they may have to be separated and reintroduced a few days later.

Siamese Fighting Fish

The Siamese Fighting Fish (*Betta splendens*) was first formally described to science in 1909. The rather drab wild form of this fish comes from the Malay Peninsula in Southeast Asia, where it lives in a wide variety of water bodies. For many hundreds of years, the male Siamese Fighting Fish has been selectively bred, resulting in the development of two distinct forms: an aggressive form with relatively short fins for *fighting*, and a much more attractive form with flowing fins for *showing* and *display*. The domestication period of the 'fighter' is indeed long, and may only be second to the Goldfish in ornamental fish circles. In the Far East, betting on the outcome of fights between two male Siamese Fighting Fish is still a very popular pastime.

Today, many tank-bred varieties of fighting fish are available, each with its own coloration and finnage. Of course, the males of these forms are much more flamboyant than their wild counterparts, and it is for this reason that a single male fighter is an attractive and fascinating addition to any community aquarium.

Fighting fish may grow to 6cm (2.4in) in length and are relatively easy to care for. They do well in a relatively warm community tank – 26-27°C (79-81°F) is ideal – that is well planted and has plenty of hiding places. Avoid extremes of pH and water hardness, and include only one male in each tank; otherwise, fights to the death may result. Fighters will thrive on a diet of good-quality flaked foods, with occasional feeds of freeze-dried foods and safe live foods.

The drab coloration and relatively short fins of the female make sexing of this fish quite easy, and the successful breeding of fighters should be within the capabilities of most aquarists. Although they can be sexed at approximately three months of age, it is best to attempt breeding with fishes that are about 9-12 months old. Allow one male to every two or three females, taking care to choose females that are at least the same size as the male.

Maintain the male fishes individually in quite small aquariums – a capacity of 2-5 litres (0.5-1 gallon) will suffice. Since fighters have a labyrinth organ, aeration is not necessary. The only regular maintenance required is to change 50-75 percent of the water each week and top up with conditioned tapwater brought to the correct temperature with a little boiling water from a kettle. Floating or sitting the small tanks in a larger, heated aquarium is a convenient way of maintaining the desired temperature.

Above: *A male red form of Siamese Fighting Fish with his bubble-nest, which he builds as a preliminary to spawning. The natural form of this species is much less colourful.*

Below: *The spawning embrace of a pair of red Siamese Fighting Fishes. The male often wraps his body fairly tightly around the female, stimulating her to release the eggs.*

73

Keep the less aggressive females together in one aquarium of 25-50 litre (5.5-11 gallon) capacity, set up and maintained as described above.

A separate breeding tank will also be required. This should be of, say, 50 litres (11 gallons) and filled to a depth of 15cm (6in) with water at a temperature of about 27°C (81°F), and certainly not below 25°C (77°F). There is no need for any tank decorations or gravel, but do include some fine-leaved plants such as *Myriophyllum* or *Cabomba*. No aeration or filtration is necessary at this stage, and the lighting should be relatively subdued.

Divide this tank in half using a clear, perforated tank divider, and introduce a mature rounded female into one half of the tank and a mature male into the other half.

The male should begin building a bubble-nest quite quickly and, once this is underway, release the plump female by removing the partition. A delicate period often follows this introduction, when the female will either be accepted by the male or rejected with a vigorous display of chasing and fin tearing. If the latter occurs, remove the female promptly and replace her with a different female, or replace the same female several days later.

Sometimes, the two fish will show no real interest in each other. If this lack of interest persists for three or four days, separate the fishes again using the divider and reintroduce them after a week or so. Alternatively, introduce a different female fish. It is important to use mature, egg-filled females, which can be recognized by their swollen appearance and the presence of a small white 'pimple' at the vent, which is actually the egg tube or ovipositor.

Fighters often spawn in the early morning, and the display and spawning sequence is fascinating to watch. At one stage the female usually lies upside-down in the water, just below the bubble-nest. The male then curls his body around his mate and the eggs are expelled and fertilized. Up to 15 eggs may result from one embrace, and this is repeated many times during a period

Above: *Siamese Fighting Fishes spawning. The eggs fall towards the bottom of the tank and are retrieved by the male. After spawning, remove the female and allow her to recuperate away from the attentions of the male. A good varied diet will help her to recover her strength.*

of a few hours to give a final brood of 200-300 eggs, although broods of 600 and more eggs have been recorded. As the eggs are shed and fertilized, they sink to the tank floor. The male fish then collects them in his mouth and spits them into the bubble-nest.

Remove the female once spawning is completed, but leave the male, as he continues to tend and guard the nest for several days. However, about three days after spawning, remove the male as well, since he may eventually eat the young.

The eggs hatch after 36-48 hours and the fry are very small. They become free swimming after five or six days, when you can feed them with infusorians or liquid fry food several times a day. After a further three or four days, the fry should be able to feed on newly hatched brineshrimp and fine dry foods before graduating on to the same food as the adult fish.

As in gouramis, the labyrinth organ begins to develop in the small fry when they are about three to four weeks old. At this time, it is vital that the air above the tank is warm and humid, and hence a glass or plastic cover is recommended. If the air is too cool, problems and possibly fish deaths may occur as a result.

As the fish grow beyond this stage, top up the tank and install some form of filtration. Foam filters are ideal, since they carry out effective yet gentle filtration, and provide aeration at the same time. Nonetheless, with broods of several hundred fishes, be sure to carry out partial water changes and make provision for splitting the fishes into further tanks, culling a certain number or disposing of them in a suitable way. And do not forget to separate the males before they mature and start fighting.

Paradisefish

The Paradisefish (*Macropodus opercularis*) comes from Southeast Asia, and is a close relative of the Dwarf Gourami and the Siamese Fighting Fish. It was first introduced to European fishkeepers in the mid-1600s, and is now available in a number of tank-bred strains.

The Paradisefish can grow to 9 or 10cm (3.5-4in) in length, the male fish being more vividly coloured and having longer fins than the female. Since the males, in particular, can be a little aggressive – both to other male Paradisefish and other fishes in a community tank – it is best to keep Paradisefish in a single-species aquarium, with only one male per tank. Otherwise, losses will occur.

Below: *Two male Paradisefishes,* Macropodus opercularis, *fighting to establish their own territories. To avoid this happening, keep only one male in a single-species aquarium.*

Above: *A male Paradisefish, building his bubble-nest. Introduce the male into the breeding tank at the same time as the female and leave them for a period of a few days.*

Right: *A typical spawning embrace of the Paradisefish. This species will tolerate a wide range of conditions and is recommended for beginners wanting to specialize in anabantoids.*

The Paradisefish tolerates a wide range of water conditions, and will feed readily on most dried and live foods. While it will live within the temperature range 15-25°C (59-77°F), a temperature of 22°C (72°F) is best for breeding.

To breed Paradisefish, introduce a mature male and a fully mature, well-rounded female into a tank of about 50 litres (11 gallons) capacity. The tank should contain some thickets of rooted plants, some floating plants and a rocky refuge or two for the female. If the fish do not spawn in a few days, remove the female and reintroduce her, or another female, after about a week or so.

The spawning and fry rearing of Paradisefish is somewhat similar to that described for the Dwarf Gourami and Siamese Fighting Fish. However, the eggs float up into the bubble-nest rather than sinking to the tank floor.

Remove the female after spawning is completed. The eggs will hatch

Right: *A breeding tank suitable for Paradisefishes. Provide plenty of cover for the female to hide from the male. Overly aggressive or amorous male anabantoids can be a problem with small or immature females.*

Above: *Paradisefishes spawning beneath the bubble-nest. The extent of the bubble-nest, and the degree to which plant material is incorporated, can vary from species to species.*

Right: *The spawning behaviour of anabantoids, such as these Paradisefishes, can be an elaborate ritual and a fascinating spectacle for proud fishkeepers to watch.*

after about 24-30 hours, but the fry will not become free swimming for several days, by which time the male should be removed. Broods of several hundred are quite common, and thus good filtration and regular partial water changes will become important as the fishes mature.

BREEDING TABLE – GOURAMIS AND THEIR

FISH SPECIES	SEXUAL CHARACTERISTICS	WATER CONDITIONS FOR BREEDING
Dwarf Gourami (Colisa lalia)	Female less brightly coloured and more rounded than male	28-30°C (82-86°F); pH around 7.0; hardness less than 7-8°dH
Chocolate Gourami (Sphaerichthys osphromenoides)	Mature female more rounded; male has light edge to fins	25-30°C (77-86°F); pH 6.0-6.5; hardness less than 5°dH
Siamese Fighting Fish (Betta splendens)	Male more colourful, with longer fins	27°C (81°F); avoid extremes of pH and hardness
Paradisefish (Macropodus opercularis)	Male more colourful, with longer fins	22°C (72°F); avoid extremes of pH and hardness

RELATIVES

SPAWNING METHOD AND BROOD CARE	NUMBER OF EGGS AND HATCHING TIME	FIRST FOOD FOR FRY
Male builds bubble-nest; he then tends eggs and young fry	Several hundred eggs; 24 hours to hatch	Green water; infusorians; liquid fry food
Female broods eggs and young fry in her mouth	Up to 80 eggs; young fry leave mother's mouth after 21 days	Newly hatched brineshrimp
Male builds and guards a bubble-nest	Several hundred eggs; 36-48 hours to hatch	Infusorians; liquid fry food
Male builds and guards a bubble-nest	Several hundred eggs; 24-30 hours to hatch	Infusorians; liquid fry food

Popular characins

The characins and related species form a large group of primarily tropical, egglaying fishes. About 1000 species have been recorded in South and Central America, with one species – the Mexican Tetra, (*Astyanax fasciatus*) – extending into the southern USA. A further 200 or so species occur in tropical Africa.

This group of fishes includes species of such diverse appearance and reputation as the piranhas (e.g. *Serrasalmus*), hatchetfishes (e.g. *Gasteropelecus*), the Blind Cave Fish (*Astyanax*) and the ever-popular shoaling tetras, such as the Neon Tetra, Cardinal Tetra and African Congo Tetra.

Neon Tetra

First desribed as *Hyphessobrycon innesi* in 1936, the Neon Tetra (now named *Paracheirodon innesi*) is surely one of the most popular of the small shoaling tetras commonly kept by aquarists. In the wild, this species is native to small streams and jungle pools in northern South America, particularly the upper Amazon region.

Below: *Characins, such as the Neon Tetra, can be bred in a well-planted tank containing soft, slightly acid water. The spawning mop featured in this set-up has been made from strands of wool, washed before use.*

Although Neon Tetras may grow to 4cm (1.6in) in the wild, the fishes offered for sale in aquarium stores are usually considerably smaller than this. Even so, a shoal of five to ten Neons in a well-planted community tank is a splendid sight, as their iridescent blue-green and red bodies catch the light like glinting jewels.

Neons are, in fact, relatively hardy fish, even tolerating quite hard and alkaline water conditions, although they do best in soft, slightly acid water. A temperature range of 20-26°C (68-79°F) is ideal for this fish, and it can be maintained in perfect health on a diet of good-quality prepared foods.

For breeding purposes, introduce five or six fish into a well-planted stock tank with subdued lighting and containing soft, slightly acid water (general hardness 1-2°dH, pH 5.5-6.0). (Producing this type of water is covered on pages 20-21.) Give the prospective parents a good varied diet, perhaps including some live food, and keep them at a steady 23-24°C (73-75°F). Be sure to provide good filtration and carry out regular partial water changes with suitably prepared water.

As the fishes develop and reach about 6-8 months of age, or 1.5-2.0cm (0.6-0.8in) in length, the female fishes will take on a more

Above: *The striking Cardinal Tetra,* Paracheirodon axelrodi, *a fish that is a little more demanding than the Neon in its breeding requirements.*

rounded appearance while the males remain noticeably slimmer. To prevent uncontrolled spawnings, segregate the sexes with a suitable tank divider, although this may not be necessary for small-scale breeding.

In order to spawn these fishes successfully, introduce a mature pair into a small tank – 30×20×20cm (12×8×8in), or even smaller – containing the same soft, slightly acid water as the stock tank, along with a generous bunch of feathery leaved plants such as *Myriophyllum* or *Cabomba*. Alternatively, use the artificial spawning 'mops' that are now available from aquatic stores, or make them from strands of well-washed wool.

Maintain the temperature at a steady 23-24°C (73-75°F) in the breeding tank, but there is no need to provide any filtration, aeration or overhead lighting; the eggs and young fry of many tetras, Neons included, are rather sensitive to bright light in the aquarium.

Introduce the pair of adult fishes into the breeding tank in the late afternoon, and their willingness to spawn may be enhanced if you place the tank where it can receive a little early morning sunshine. If all goes well, the male fish will soon begin displaying to the female, leading or driving her through the plants or spawning mop. It is here that the eggs are released by the female and fertilized by the male. The eggs, perhaps a few dozen in all, are laid in bursts, some sticking to the plants, others falling to the tank floor.

Immediately after spawning, the adult fish lose interest in each other. Remove them from the breeding tank at this stage, since Neons are quite avid egg eaters. Left alone, the eggs will hatch in a shaded tank after about 24 hours, and the fry become free swimming three to four days later. At this time, offer them small but frequent meals of infusorians or liquid fry food, and by the time they are a week old they should accept newly hatched brineshrimp. Later, they will graduate on to powdered baby fish foods and fine flaked foods.

Partial water changes of 25 percent each week are a good idea, and when the fry are about two months old transfer them to a larger tank with gentle but efficient filtration. Given plenty of space and good water quality, they will grow rapidly. Once again, it is vital to provide a varied diet (without overfeeding) and to make regular, partial water changes. As soon as the fry are more than a few weeks old, you can gradually replace the soft, acid water with harder water, if this is more convenient.

Cardinal Tetra
The scientific name of the Cardinal Tetra is *Paracheirodon axelrodi*, and it was first described in 1956 in honour of the famous American fishkeeper and scientist Dr. Herbert R. Axelrod. With its electric blue back and vivid red belly, it is even more attractive than the Neon Tetra. It is also rather more demanding when it comes to breeding, however.

It is a native of northern South America, especially the basin of the Rio Negro, and in the wild may reach 4cm (1.6in) in length, although aquarium specimens are usually smaller than this. The Cardinal Tetra is another 'soft water' species. Thus, to maintain and breed it successfully in the aquarium, try to ensure that the temperature and water quality conditions closely match those described for the Neon Tetra.

However, greater success at spawning Cardinal Tetras has been reported at a pH value of 6.0-6.5 and a general hardness value of 3-4° dH. Both these figures are slightly higher than those mentioned for the Neon. When breeding Cardinal Tetras (and also Neons) be sure to use one of the blackwater tonics as a spawning aid.

Although generally more delicate and fussy over water conditions, the selection and care of prospective Cardinal Tetra parents, and the care of the eggs and young fry, are all similar to that described for Neon Tetras. Notably, however, the eggs and fry of Cardinal Tetras are particularly sensitive to bright light. The fry are also quite slow growing and can be rather difficult to rear. They are very sensitive to sudden changes in water quality and hence it is a good idea to monitor pH value, hardness and even nitrite or ammonia levels regularly.

When the fry are six to eight weeks old, move them to a larger, rearing tank containing the same soft, acid water as they are used to. To keep conditions in the rearing tank as hygienic as possible for the growing fish, install a gentle but efficient filter.

Using similar methods, a number of other popular tetras may be spawned in the aquarium, including *Hemigrammus* species (such as the Glowlight Tetra, *H.erythrozonus*) and *Hyphessobrycon* species (such as the Rosy Tetra, *H.rosaceus*, the Serpae Tetra, *H.serpae*, and also the Lemon Tetra, *H.pulchripinnis*).

Congo Tetra
The Congo Tetra (*Phenacogrammus interruptus* or, as it is sometimes known, *Micralestes interruptus*) is a very beautiful Central African shoaling characin. The Congo Tetra is, however, quite a bit larger than the Neon or Cardinal Tetra, with the male fish reaching 8cm (3.2in) and the females about 6cm (2.4in) in length.

Both sexes have an iridescent hue to their flanks and quite flowing fins. However, the coloration and finnage of the male fish is particularly pronounced, with extended rays in the dorsal and caudal fins that give them a fringed appearance.

In common with the Cardinal Tetra, the Congo Tetra also prefers soft, acid water conditions, especially if it is

BREEDING TABLE – TETRAS

FISH SPECIES	SEXUAL CHARACTERISTICS	WATER CONDITIONS FOR BREEDING
Neon Tetra (*Paracheirodon innesi*)	Male slimmer than more rounded female	23-24°C (73-75°F); pH 5.5-6.0; hardness 1-2°dH
Cardinal Tetra (*Paracheirodon axelrodi*)	Male slimmer than more rounded female	23-24°C (73-75°F); pH 6.0-6.5; hardness 3-4°dH
Congo Tetra (*Phenacogrammus interruptus*)	Male larger, with more flowing fins	25°C (77°F); pH 6-7; hardness less than 3 or 4°dH

Above: *A fine pair of Congo Tetras* (Phenacogrammus interruptus*), the larger male showing the typically extended dorsal and caudal fins. This species breeds well in soft, peaty, slightly acidic water.*

to thrive, develop its finnage to the full, and also breed. A pH value between 6 and 7 and a general hardness value below 3 or 4°dH, together with a steady temperature of about 25°C (77°F), are all recommended. Since this species really does like peaty, 'blackwater' conditions, regular use

of a blackwater tonic is also a good idea. The Congo Tetra adapts well to prepared diets such as flaked foods, but also appears to enjoy occasional supplies of a safe live food.

In order to breed the Congo Tetra, set up a 60-100cm (24-39in) aquarium with plenty of plants but some free-swimming space, containing water of the quality described above. Into this introduce, say, two females and four males, choosing individuals that are fully grown and about 12 months of age. If all goes well, an active courtship will ensue, with each female scattering up to 300 eggs over the tank floor. The eggs are not adhesive and have quite a long incubation period of up to six days. A day or two after spawning, transfer the adult fishes to a separate aquarium, perhaps segregating the sexes to allow recuperation and to prevent indiscriminate spawnings.

Once hatched, the Congo fry become free swimming after a further two or three days and can be fed on newly hatched brineshrimp, soon graduating on to powdered baby fish foods and, eventually, the same food as the parent fishes.

SPAWNING METHOD AND BROOD CARE	NUMBER OF EGGS AND HATCHING TIME	FIRST FOOD FOR FRY
Eggs laid among plants; remove parents after spawning	Several dozen eggs; 24 hours to hatch	Infusorians; liquid fry food
Eggs laid among plants; remove parents after spawning	Several dozen eggs; 24 hours to hatch	Infusorians; liquid fry food
Eggs dropped over tank floor; remove parents after spawning	Up to 300; 6 days to hatch	Newly hatched brineshrimp

Barbs, danios and rasboras

The Minnow or Carp family (the Cyprinidae) is the largest single family of fishes, with over 1600 species. While cyprinids such as the carps (e.g. *Cyprinus, Carassius*), the Roach (*Rutilus*) and the Dace or Orfe (*Leuciscus*), are the dominant fish species in many freshwater habitats in Europe and Asia, other species of cyprinids also occur in North America and Africa. However, within the tropical and subtropical regions of Asia and, to a lesser extent, Africa, barbs, danios and rasboras are the commonly encountered cyprinids, and many of the smaller species are now firm aquarium favourites.

Barbs

While some barbs, such as the Indian Mahseer (*Barbus tor*), can grow to a staggering 2 metres (6.5ft) in length – and form an important local food source in some areas – it is the more diminutive forms such as the Tiger Barb that are frequently kept by aquarists around the world.

The Tiger or Sumatran Barb (*Barbus tetrazona tetrazona*) originates from the Southeast Asian islands of Borneo and Sumatra, as well as mainland Indonesia, where it lives in a wide variety of still and flowing waters. The characteristic striped body and red finnage of this fish is familiar to most aquarists. It may reach a length of 6-7cm (2.4-2.8in), but is usually smaller than this in the aquarium. Sexing can sometimes be a little difficult, although the mature female is usually noticeably plumper than the male, and there is usually less colour to her dorsal and anal fin.

In the community tank, Tiger Barbs are quite tolerant of a wide variety of water conditions, and will flourish at any temperature in the range 20-25°C (68-77°F). This species has a reputation for being a little aggressive towards other fish, especially those with long trailing fins. This may be offset to some extent by keeping Tiger Barbs in shoals of five or more individuals, and by keeping them in a medium-sized to large well-planted aquarium. In the home aquarium,

Below: *A conditioning tank suitable for Tiger Barbs. A male and female should be conditioned for breeding on either side of a tank divider. Feed both on a good varied diet, including some of the safe live foods.*

they thrive on a diet of good-quality flake foods, although occasional feeds of freeze-dried foods are also a good idea. Naturally, a good, varied diet of nutritious foods is essential to encourage successful breeding.

As with most aquarium fishes, it is best to breed Tiger Barbs in a separate tank. Make this quite large to allow for the rather vigorous courtship behaviour of these fish. Consequently, avoid tanks less than 60cm (24in) long or about 50 litres

Above: *The Tiger Barb,* Barbus tetrazona, *easily recognizable by its four stripes. These active shoaling fishes need a spacious tank in which to perform their vigorous courtship and spawning manoeuvres.*

(11 gallons) in capacity. You will need a minimum of two tanks of at least this size; one divided into two with a perforated tank divider and to be used to condition the males and females for spawning, and one undivided tank for the spawning process itself.

Set up each of these tanks along fairly spartan lines: a foam filter in one corner; one or two dense clumps of feathery plants (e.g. *Cabomba* or *Myriophyllum*) weighted to the tank floor; and a sheet of transparent plastic or glass as a tank cover. Use soft and slightly acid water (general hardness 5-8° dH, pH around 6.5) in both these tanks, heated to a steady 26-27°C (79-81°F). The willingness of the fish to spawn may be increased by the regular use of a blackwater tonic. (See also page 15.)

Having conditioned the adult male and female fishes on separate sides of the divider in one tank – using a good varied diet and perhaps including a little safe live food – transfer the brood pair to the undivided spawning tank during the early evening. The following day, there should be some signs of activity in the tank, with the colours of the male fish, especially the fins, deepening noticeably. Spawning usually occurs on day two or three in the breeding tank, with the male fish vigorously chasing the female all around the tank and the pair diving through the clump of plants. Once spawning is complete, the exhausted fishes will rest on the tank floor. Remove them immediately at this stage, since they are voracious egg eaters. Also, separate the male and female so that they can recuperate.

The eggs will be seen stuck to the plants or to the tank floor. They usually hatch after 36 hours, but the newly hatched fry continue to hang motionless on the spawning medium for another day or so. About three or four days after spawning, the fry should appear at the water surface and it is now that you should offer food for the first time. Frequent small meals of newly hatched brineshrimp and finely powdered foods are ideal.

The water in the tank should remain clear and sweet smelling at all times. Careful feeding and regular partial water changes are both important, especially as the young fishes begin to grow. Since the female Tiger Barb can lay several hundred eggs, there can be large numbers of baby fish to care for. As the fish grow, they soon accept the same food as their parents, but regular thinning or culling of their numbers will be required to maintain good growth and healthy development.

Other barbs that may be bred under similar conditions include the Rosy Barb (*Barbus conchonius*), Cuming's Barb (*Barbus cumingi*), the Ruby Barb (*Barbus nigrofasciatus*) and the Green Barb (*Barbus semifasciolatus*).

Danios

A number of danios are kept as community tank fish, including the Pearl Danio (*Brachydanio albolineatus*), the Zebra Danio (*Brachydanio rerio*) and the Giant Danio (*Danio malabaricus*). All are hardy, peaceful, easy-care fishes and, although quite closely related to the barbs, they are best spawned under slightly different conditions.

Separate the male and female fishes – the female is much more

Above: *Tiger Barbs spawning. These fishes usually lay their eggs among fine-leaved plants, although spawning mops can be used. After spawning, remove the adult fishes to prevent them eating their own eggs.*

rounded than the male – and condition them for spawning as described for Tiger Barbs (see page 85). During this time, set up a shallower spawning tank containing about 10cm (4in) of water heated to a steady 28-29°C (82-84°F). Place a layer of washed marbles or similarly sized pebbles on the tank floor, and add a small clump of *Myriophyllum* or similar aquatic plant. Gently aerate the water in this tank using a fine mist airstone. Water conditions for spawning danios are not as critical as they are for barbs, and anything around a pH value of 7 with a general hardness not exceeding 15°dH will usually suffice.

Once the segregated adult fishes have been conditioned on a good varied diet for about two to three weeks, introduce a shoal with a ratio of three males to two females into the spawning tank. Over the ensuing few days they should spawn, their scattered eggs falling in-between the marbles or pebbles on the tank floor. Here, they will be well out of reach of the parents, which are avid egg eaters, in common with the barbs.

Above: *A breeding set-up ideal for danios. Many danios spawn in a shoal, and will eat their own eggs if they do not fall to safety between* pebbles or marbles. Shallow water in the breeding tank lessens the opportunities for egg eating, by reducing the distance the eggs fall.

Although the eggs hatch after about 24 hours, the young fry remain in the bottom substrate for a further four or five days before they become free swimming. Consequently, the parent fishes can be left in the breeding tank for a few days after spawning, without any harm coming to the eggs or fry.

A mature female danio may lay several hundred eggs and as the fry become free swimming be sure to provide frequent small feeds of liquid fry food, infusorians, newly hatched brineshrimp and, eventually, finely powdered and crumbled dried foods. As the fish grow, top up the spawning tank with conditioned tapwater and install a foam filter. Regular partial water changes will help to maintain satisfactory conditions in the tank.

Below: *A pair of Pearl Danios,* Brachydanio albolineatus. *The slimmer male is below the more rounded female. This is an excellent fish for the novice fish breeder. Follow the guidelines given for danios.*

Above: *The White Cloud Mountain Minnow* (Tanichthys albonubes) *is a hardy egglayer that will thrive in an unheated aquarium or in an outdoor pool during the summer months.*

Below: *White Cloud Mountain Minnows spawning among fine-leaved plants. Each female lays 50-100 eggs, which hatch after 24 hours. These fishes are less avid egg eaters.*

White Cloud Mountain Minnow

The White Cloud Mountain Minnow (*Tanichthys albonubes*) is another cyprinid fish that can be spawned in the same way as the danios. First seen by aquarists in the late 1930s, this fish became known as the 'poor man's Neon'. It comes from the mountains around Canton in China, and also occurs in the region of Hong Kong, where it lives in shoals in local streams.

In the wild, water temperatures may fluctuate between 14 and 25°C (57-77°F), and so do not keep this fish too warm in the aquarium. A maximum summer temperature of 20-22°C (68-72°F) is satisfactory, although a winter decrease in temperature to around 16-18°C (61-64°F) will cause no harm, and may actually be beneficial. Consequently, White Cloud Mountain Minnows are ideal for an indoor, unheated aquarium. They can also be kept in an outside pool or aquarium during the summer months.

This fish grows to a maximum length of 4cm (1.6in) and can be bred as a pair or in a small shoal in a well-planted aquarium. The males are slimmer and more brightly coloured than the females, and neither parent displays the same pronounced egg-eating tendencies characteristic of many of the danios.

The slightly sticky eggs are laid among feathery leaved plants, perhaps 50-100 per female. These

hatch after about 24 hours, and the fry become free swimming after a further five or six days. One strategy is simply to leave the parent fishes in the breeding tank, carefully removing the tiny fry from between the plants with a fine net or ladle. Rear these on using liquid fry food or newly hatched brineshrimp as soon as they become free swimming. They soon graduate on to finely powdered dried foods and, eventually, the same flaked and safe live foods as their parents.

Frequent partial water changes, good aeration and not too high a temperature are all important in the successful breeding and rearing of White Cloud Mountain Minnows.

Rasboras

The rasboras form a group of some 50 species of fishes from East Africa and southern and eastern Asia, extending into Indonesia and the Philippines. They are generally small shoaling fishes that abound in flowing and still waters, notably the former.

The rasboras are ideal fishes for a well-planted community aquarium, where a shoal of 5-10 individuals can be particularly attractive as they swim actively through the mid to upper regions of the water. A temperature around 25°C (77°F) is satisfactory, but be sure to avoid using particularly hard and alkaline water. Rasboras will feed readily on a range of good-quality dried foods, although the use of freeze-dried and safe live foods is

Above: *This breeding set-up will suit the rasboras. Use soft water filtered through peat (or add a blackwater tonic) and include some broad-leaved plants as spawning sites. A reasonably small tank will suffice.*

recommended, especially when conditioning the adults for breeding.

While most rasboras are not particularly easy to breed, some are more difficult than others. Some species, such as the Scissortail

Below: *The Harlequin,* Rasbora heteromorpha, *usually lays its eggs on the underside of a leaf, but not always, as this photograph shows! Try to provide peaceful conditions for this species to breed sucessfully.*

Above: *This is the more usual spawning behaviour of the Harlequin, i.e. laying eggs on the underside of a broad leaf. Keep lighting levels low.*

(*Rasbora trilineata*), the Black-striped Rasbora (*R. taeniata*), and the Side-striped Rasbora (*R.lateristriata*), can be bred in the same way as barbs. Soft, slightly acid water and the regular use of a blackwater tonic, (or filtration of the water through aquarium peat), will help to encourage breeding success.

Some rasboras lay up to several hundred eggs, but the smaller aquarium varieties usually produce less than 100 per female. Many of these fishes will breed in quite small aquariums (down to 30cm/12in), as long as the correct water quality conditions are provided.

BREEDING TABLE – BARBS, DANIOS AND

FISH SPECIES	SEXUAL CHARACTERISTICS	WATER CONDITIONS FOR BREEDING
Tiger Barb (*Barbus tetrazona tetrazona*)	Mature female more plump and less colourful in fins than male	26-27°C (79-81°F); pH 6.5; hardness 5-8°dH
Various danios (*Brachydanio, Danio*)	Female more rounded than male	28-29°C (82-84°F); avoid extremes of pH and hardness
White Cloud Mountain Minnow (*Tanichthys albonubes*)	Male slimmer and more colourful than female	18-20°C (64-68°F); avoid extremes of pH and hardness
Harlequin (*Rasbora heteromorpha*)	Female more rounded than male	28°C (82°F); pH 5.5; hardness 1-3°dH

Although very popular, the Harlequin (*Rasbora heteromorpha*) is in some ways a rather atypical rasbora, and one of the more difficult-to-breed species. The Harlequin comes from Indonesia, Sumatra and Thailand, where it lives in marshy pools and overgrown streams. It grows to a maximum length of 4.5cm (1.8in) and is a peaceful, shoaling fish that makes a lively addition to any well-planted community aquarium.

Soft, acid water (general hardness 1-3°dh, pH 5.5) is important for the successful breeding of the Harlequin, as is the use of peat-filtered water or a blackwater tonic. After conditioning the male and female fishes as described for barbs, introduce an obviously mature female and a male into a 30cm (12in) tank furnished with one or two potted, flat-leaved plants (e.g. *Cryptocoryne*), and containing water of suitable quality heated to approximately 28°C (82°F). Rasboras in general, and Harlequins in particular, prefer peace and quiet for breeding and low lighting levels.

Leave the prospective parents together for up to a week. If they have not spawned in that time, separate them and reintroduce them at a later date. Alternatively, introduce a different pair into the breeding tank.

Once spawning has occurred, as indicated by the slimness of the female fish, remove both parents from the breeding tank. The eggs, laid on the underside of the flat leaves, will hatch after 24-30 hours. Up to 250 eggs are produced by each female, and the resultant fry become free swimming after three to five days. At this stage offer them small but frequent meals of liquid fry food, infusorians and newly hatched brineshrimp. As the fry grow, carry out regular partial water changes, install a good filtration system and prepare to thin out their numbers.

RASBORAS

SPAWNING METHOD AND BROOD CARE	NUMBER OF EGGS AND HATCHING TIME	FIRST FOOD FOR FRY
Eggs laid among plants or on tank floor; remove parents after spawning	Several hundred eggs; 36 hours to hatch	Newly hatched brineshrimp; finely powdered dried foods
Eggs usually laid on tank floor; remove parents after spawning	Several hundred eggs; 24 hours to hatch	Infusorians; liquid fry food; newly hatched brineshrimp
Eggs laid among plants	50-100 eggs; 24 hours to hatch	Newly hatched brineshrimp
Eggs laid on underside of leaves of aquarium plants	Up to 250 eggs; 24-30 hours to hatch	Infusorians; liquid fry food; newly hatched brineshrimp

Catfishes

Catfishes form a collection of 30 or so families of freshwater and marine fishes, encompassing approximately 2000 species, 1200 of which are found in South America. They are usually easily recognized by their whiskery snouts containing one to four pairs of barbels. However, catfishes are very diverse, ranging from giants, such as the European wels (*Silurus*) that may grow to 5 metres (over 16ft) in length and weigh 300kg (660lb), to the comparatively miniscule South American species that rarely grow any longer than 2 or 3cm (0.8-1.2in).

It is these small South American catfishes that are particularly popular among aquarists, notably members of the *Corydoras* (mailed catfish) genus. There are over 100 species of *Corydoras* catfishes, but less than a quarter of these are well known as aquarium subjects. These peaceful, active fishes are ideal inmates for the community aquarium, where they do best as a small shoal, rather than singly or in pairs.

Corydoras catfish

Corydoras catfishes live in fairly fast-flowing rivers in central and northern South America. They will thrive in an aquarium of any size at a temperature of 20-25°C (68-77°F) and with a sandy substrate. There is no need for the tank to be heavily planted. Although they are not especially fussy over water conditions, it appears that they flourish in softish, neutral to slightly acid water. Certainly, avoid extremes of pH and water hardness, and be sure to provide good aeration and filtration.

Although scavengers by nature, it is not enough to leave these fish to survive on the food remains left by other fishes in the aquarium. Feed *Corydoras* catfishes on good-quality tablet foods, with occasional feeds of flaked, freeze-dried and safe, 'wormy' live foods. Breeding success can be achieved only by providing a correct diet.

These fish *are* difficult to sex. When viewed from above, the female body contour is widest at the point of the pectoral fins; the male's body is widest at a point *behind* the pectoral fins. The female has a more rounded belly, which is also more pink, than the male. In some species, the male has a higher dorsal fin.

As far as is known, most of the *Corydoras* catfishes breed in a similar fashion, and given correct tank conditions, species such as *C.paleatus* (Peppered Catfish) and *C.aeneus* (Bronze Catfish) are reasonably easy to breed.

Below: *This tank set-up is ideal for spawning* Corydoras *catfishes. Use a foam cartridge filter, and ensure that the water is not too hard and alkaline. The rocks, plants or tank glass will be used as spawning sites after careful cleaning. Feed these catfishes on a diet of tablet foods, plus occasional meals of 'wormy' livefoods.*

It is best to attempt breeding in a special tank set up as follows. Use a 45×25×25cm (18×10×10in) tank, or a slightly larger one, furnished with a covering of fine, well-washed gravel on the floor and one or two small rocks, plus one or two Amazon Swordplants in pots. Provide filtration by means of a foam filter, left running for 18-24 hours a day. Using such a filter, additional aeration will be unnecessary. Cover the tank with a sheet of glass or transparent plastic, and keep the water at a steady 23-24°C (73-75°F). Since *Corydoras* do not like hard, alkaline conditions, steer clear of calcium- and magnesium-containing rocks and gravel. In areas where the tapwater is very hard or alkaline, condition it by dilution with clean rainwater or by allowing it to stand in contact with aquarium peat. (See page 20 for more details on conditioning tapwater.)

Such a tank will be suitable for a trio of two males and one female, or up to five males and three females. When attempting to breed *Corydoras* catfishes, it is common to have a surplus of male fishes.

These fishes often indicate their readiness to breed by periods of increased activity and by the female fish carefully cleaning possible spawning sites, such as rocks, plant leaves, the glass of the tank, etc. Immediately before spawning, the female fish presses her mouth to the vent of the male. In this fashion, she obtains the milt and conveys it to the selected spawning site. Here she releases it and immediately lays a small number of eggs. *Corydoras* catfishes may lay up to 150-200 eggs, with the spawning process taking place over one or two days. The eggs are large and easy to see.

The adult fishes may spawn again in a week or so, but may also go for long periods without spawning. In the wild, there may be a seasonal cycle to spawning activity, which is maintained in the aquarium. It

Below: Corydoras *catfishes are often spawned in a group containing more males than females, as shown here. This is the first photograph in a spawning sequence that is continued and concluded on the next page.*

BREEDING TABLE – CATFISHES

FISH SPECIES	SEXUAL CHARACTERISTICS	WATER CONDITIONS FOR BREEDING
Corydoras catfishes	Female more rounded; male with higher dorsal fin	23-24°C (73-75°F); avoid hard, alkaline water

Above left: The catfishes lay their eggs on a flat surface, often the glass of the aquarium. The large eggs take 3-5 days to hatch.

Above: The female catfish lays her eggs into a 'cup' formed by her pelvic fins, and may then take them to the chosen spawning site.

Left: Each female may lay up to 200 eggs, encouraged by the attendant males. Removing infertile and fungussed eggs is quite easy.

appears that fishes reluctant to spawn may be induced to do so by temporarily cooling the breeding tank, by floating a few ice cubes in the water or by carrying out a partial water change with cooler water. However, do not suddenly decrease the temperature by more than 4°C (18°F) in this way.

When the adult fishes have spawned, remove them from the breeding tank or they may eat the eggs and/or the fry. The eggs will hatch after three to five days and the resultant fry are very small. In fact, the only indication that the eggs have hatched may be the empty egg cases remaining. The fry continue feeding on their yolk sacs for about 24 hours, when you should offer them small, frequent feeds of newly hatched brineshrimp and finely powdered dry foods. They will grow quickly, eventually taking the same food as their parents. With sensible feeding, good filtration and regular partial water changes, the fry should reach a length of 1cm (0.4in) in a period of three to four months.

Sometimes, one or two of the eggs will turn white and show signs of fungal attack. In this situation, treat the water in the breeding tank with a proprietary antifungal preparation (see the disease section, page 31).

SPAWNING METHOD AND BROOD CARE	NUMBER OF EGGS AND HATCHING TIME	FIRST FOOD FOR FRY
Eggs laid on flat surface	Up to 200 eggs; 3-5 days to hatch	Newly hatched brineshrimp; finely powdered dried foods

Common livebearers

The vast majority of fishes are egglayers, and reproduce by the female shedding her eggs into the water, where they are fertilized by milt (sperm) from the male. The degree of protection provided for the eggs by the parent fishes may then vary from non-existent, as in most characins, to extensive brood care, as in many cichlids. In some fishes, however, the eggs are fertilized *inside* the female, following mating with the male.

Internal fertilization, and the subsequent development of the eggs inside the body of the mother fish, affords them excellent protection from predators and adverse environmental conditions, and usually results in the eventual production of a relatively small number of well-developed offspring.

Livebearing, in one form or another, is seen in the true Sharks and Rays, the Coelacanth (*Latimeria*) and in such familiar tropical aquarium fishes as the Goodeids, the Halfbeaks (Hemirhamphidae), the Four-eyed Fish (*Anableps*), and the ever-popular livebearing toothcarps – the Guppies, Platies, Swordtails and Mollies, which all belong to the family Poecilidae.

Below: *The anal fin of male livebearers is modified into an elongated 'gonopodium', which is used for transferring milt (sperm) to the female for internal fertilization.*

Bottom: *The female livebearer is usually rotund, with a rounded anal fin. A dark spot on the belly near the vent shows that she is mature.*

Guppy or Millions Fish

The Guppy (*Poecilia reticulata*) is a livebearing fish originally from South America, north of the Amazon, but which is now almost worldwide in its distribution. It has, in fact, been introduced into a number of countries to control disease-carrying mosquitoes (by eating the larvae).

Male Guppies may reach up to 3.5cm (1.4in) in length, while the female is usually considerably larger when fully grown, at up to 6cm (2.4in). Adult male fishes usually have a more developed, more highly coloured tail fin and an elongated and pointed anal fin, the 'gonopodium'. The gonopodium is used in the transfer of milt from the male to the female fish, and is therefore relatively long and pointed, compared to the more rounded anal fin of the female fish.

In nature, Guppies are found in still or gently flowing waters, both fresh and brackish, which probaby accounts (in part) for the hardiness of the fishes in captivity. However, Guppies are not as hardy as some people imagine. They thrive in a large well-planted tank with a steady temperature within the range 20-25°C (68-77°F). They do appear a little sensitive to sudden changes in temperature, and to very soft water. In the aquarium, it is advisable to feed them on a good varied diet, including high-quality flaked foods (including vegetable-based flake), plus freeze-dried foods and the occasional safe live foods (see page 29).

Many aquarists keep one or two pairs of Guppies in their community tank, but then realize that the young fish are often eaten by their parents or other fishes before they can be rescued and transferred to another tank. Therefore, the best approach is to remove the pregnant female from the community tank as soon as she starts to swell with developing young and place her in a small breeding tank, say 30x20x20cm (12x10x10in) in size. Furnish this tank with a thin covering of aquarium gravel on the floor (although this is not essential) and generous bunches of fine-leaved plants (e.g. *Cabomba*). Heat it to the same temperature as the community tank and fit a cover. At this stage, filtration and/or aeration are not essential, but bearing in mind that the female fish can 'drop' 20-200 young at one go, filtration (especially) may become necessary when the fry begin to grow. A foam filter and regular partial water changes will keep conditions in the breeding tank healthy as the fry begin to grow, although there will come a time when

Below: *Many livebearers will breed in a community aquarium, but a breeding tank with fine-leaved plants is recommended for the serious hobbyist. Model such a tank on the arrangement shown here.*

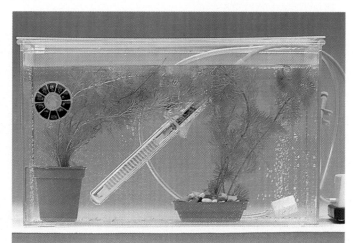

Above: *A pair of Guppies,* Poecilia reticulata. *The more colourful male has longer fins than the drab but considerably larger female. The difference in the shape of the anal fin is quite clearly visible here.*

some of the brood will have to be disposed of – to fellow aquarists or to your local pet store.

The time taken from mating to birth is between three and five weeks, depending on the water temperature. It is important not to handle the female too near the time she is due to give birth or she may abort the young. After she has dropped her young, transfer her to another tank, preferably away from the attentions of male Guppies, for several days of rest and recuperation.

The young fry will willingly feed on newly hatched brineshrimp, finely powdered dried foods and, eventually, suitable adult foods.

If you cannot provide a separate tank for the pregnant (gravid) female to give birth in, you may like to use one of the widely available plastic 'breeding traps'. However, some of these are really too small for a large female livebearer and her resultant brood of fry, and as the fry grow the problem of where to house them safely still remains. Therefore, a separate breeding or 'delivery' tank, which can subsequently double as a fry-rearing tank, is recommended for livebearers such as Guppies.

Below: *Heavily gravid female livebearers can be moved gently into a breeding trap, shown here floating in a well-planted tank. The young drop through perforations to the safety of a separate chamber.*

Platies, Swordtails and Mollies

The Platies and Swordtails (*Xiphophorus*) and the Mollies (*Poecilia*) are all close relatives of the Guppy and come from Central and northeastern South America, with their range extending into North America and the West Indies.

Rather like the Guppy, they are available in a vast array of tank-bred forms, although there are also quite a number of naturally occurring species. The latter have a more subtle appeal when compared to the highly coloured or elaborately finned domesticated forms.

These livebearers require a steady temperature in the range 23-26°C (73-79°F). Perhaps temperatures a little higher will suit the Mollies such as the Black Molly, which can develop a number of diseases if kept in water that is too cool. The Platies, Swords and Mollies are ideally suited to a community tank, where groups of

Below: A pair of Black Mollies, an extremely popular livebearer. It should be possible to distinguish the sexes from a few weeks of age, when the anal fin of the male has taken on its typical, elongated appearance.

one male to two or three females will often do well and even breed. Avoid an excess of male fishes since squabbles may result.

All of these fish thrive in a well-planted aquarium. Indeed, lush plant growth is essential if many of the fry are to survive in a community tank. For breeding purposes, a good varied diet is essential, and should include a vegetable-based flaked food and the occasional safe live food.

Platies, Swordtails and Mollies are quite hardy fish, but that is no excuse for providing them with substandard aquarium conditions. They will do well in most types of water, so long as it is not too soft or acidic. Many of the Mollies appear to benefit from the addition of a little aquarium or marine salt to the water (0.5-1gm per litre/0.5-1 teaspoonful per gallon); ensure that this salt level is maintained at every partial water change, of course.

Sexing the adult fishes, their breeding and the subsequent rearing of the fry should all follow the guidelines set out for the Guppy, except that Swordtails, Platies and especially Mollies do prefer the water a little warmer and benefit from the addition of a small amount of salt.

Mature male Swordtails are easily distinguished by the possession of a pronounced 'sword' on the lower edge of their tail fin, which gives the fish its common name. Once again, for Platies, Swordtails and Mollies, a separate breeding or 'delivery' tank is recommended in preference to a 'breeding trap' for the pregnant female, and this tank can then be used for rearing the offspring. Good filtration, regular partial water changes and the eventual thinning of the growing fry are all important when rearing these fishes.

The line breeding of selected strains of Guppies, Platies, Swordtails and Mollies is complicated by the fact that these fishes can mature at a very early age, perhaps only a few weeks, and will often interbreed with each other. The fertilized female can store milt from the male fish in her body and use it to fertilize at least five successive batches of eggs in the absence of the male. Therefore, in any sort of controlled breeding programme, it is vital to separate the male and female fish as soon as it is possible to distinguish the sexes. If you are in any doubt about the sex of a fish, always put the unconfirmed sexed fish into the *males'* tank. This will prevent any male getting into the females' tank and ruining the strain.

Sex reversal in Swordtails

The reproductive habits of the livebearing fishes are particularly interesting, and have attracted the attention of scientists across the

Above: *A female Swordtail giving birth to one of up to 200 fully formed young that she may produce in a single breeding cycle.*

world. In the Swordtail (*Xiphophorus helleri*), in particular, the phenomenon of sex reversal has been frequently noted by scientists and hobbyists.

In most higher animals, the sex of each individual is determined at the moment of fertilization of the egg. However, this is not the case with the Swordtail. Each immature fish could develop into a male *or* a female, depending on whether the male or the female reproductive organs develop first. If the ovaries (female reproductive organs) develop first, these will secrete female hormones and the fish will develop into a female; the opposite occurs if the male testes develop first. Later on in life, however, if the female ovaries regress and cease to function, the once female fish can turn into a functional male.

Female to male changes are not uncommon, but male to female changes have rarely, if ever, been observed in Swordtails. Also of interest is the fact that external factors such as pH can affect the sexual development of some fishes. It has been shown that at low (acid) pH values (around pH 5-6) a greater proportion of male fish develop in the broods of the Swordtail, and also in many dwarf cichlids. At higher (alkaline) pH values (pH 7+), the sex ratio within the broods of these fishes is weighted towards the females.

Halfbeak

The Halfbeak (*Dermogenys pusillus*) is a freshwater relative of the marine flying fish. The halfbeak family contains more than 60 species, although it is *Dermogenys pusillus* from Southeast Asia that is most often kept by aquarists. This rather shy livebearing fish does not mix too well in a community tank, and hence should be kept only with other similarly timid species.

For breeding purposes, set up a separate 50-100 litre (11-22 gallon) aquarium containing a male and two females. Male Halfbeaks are usually much smaller than the females, and have a 'folded' anal fin and are generally slimmer. Having two males in the same aquarium often leads to squabbles, whereas providing two females will allow one to rest while the male is chasing the other.

Include some floating plants in the breeding tank and keep it at a

Below: *The Halfbeak is a rather aggressive fish. Keep only one male in a small breeding tank, with some floating plants to afford the female a refuge from the male's attentions. Since Halfbeaks are good jumpers, be sure to cover the tank securely.*

temperature of around 26°C (79°F). Be sure to cover it with a tight-fitting lid, since Halfbeaks are good jumpers, and provide filtration and aeration by means of a foam filter. Avoid extremes of pH, although some aquarists have found that adding a little aquarium salt (0.5-1.5gm per litre/0.5-1.5 teaspoonsful per gallon) is beneficial to the fishes.

Offer the fishes a good varied diet, particularly live food, such as bloodworm and floating insects, although they may take dried foods. Feed worms to the fish using a floating worm-feeder, as their characteristic (and unique) jaw structure inhibits them from feeding from lower levels in the water.

The time taken between mating and the birth of the live young is about 40-45 days, with broods of 10-20 young being common. Ideally, move the pregnant female to another small aquarium to give birth, otherwise the young may be eaten by the parents. After she has dropped her young, transfer her back to the main tank.

Rear the fry on newly hatched brineshrimp and, eventually, the same food as their parents. The characteristic 'half beak' will appear at about four or five weeks of age.

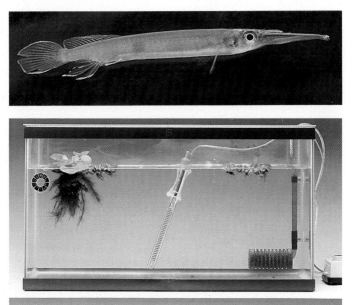

BREEDING TABLE – LIVEBEARERS

FISH SPECIES	SEXUAL CHARACTERISTICS	WATER CONDITIONS FOR BREEDING
Guppy or Millions Fish *(Poecilia reticulata)*	Male fish smaller with more flowing tail fin, and pointed anal fin or 'gonopodium'	20-25°C (68-77°F); avoid very soft water
Platy *(Xiphophorus maculatus)*	Male smaller and slimmer with gonopodium	23-26°C (73-79°F); avoid very soft water
Swordtail *(Xiphophorus helleri)*	Male usually smaller and slimmer with gonopodium and pronounced sword on tail	23-26°C (73-79°F); avoid very soft water
Black Molly *(Poecilia sp.)*	Male fish with gonopodium and is often smaller and slimmer	23-26°C (73-79°F); add aquarium salt at 0.5-1gm/litre (0.5-1 teaspoon per gallon)
Sailfin Molly *(Poecilia latipinna)*	Male fish with gonopodium and is often smaller and slimmer	23-26°C (73-79°F); add aquarium salt at 0.5-1gm/litre (0.5-1 teaspoon per gallon)
Velifera Molly *(Poecilia velifera)*	Male fish with gonopodium and is often smaller and slimmer	23-26°C (73-79°F); add aquarium salt at 0.5-1gm/litre (0.5-1 teaspoon per gallon)
Halfbeak *(Dermogenys pusillus)*	Male smaller and slimmer with 'folded' anal fin	26°C (79°F); avoid extremes of pH and hardness; add aquarium salt at 0.5-1.5gm/litre (0.5-1.5 teaspoons per gallon)

PERIOD BETWEEN MATING AND BIRTH	NUMBER OF YOUNG PER BROOD	FIRST FOOD
21-35 days	20-200	Newly hatched brineshrimp; finely powdered dried foods
28-42 days	10-80 or more	Newly hatched brineshrimp; finely powdered dried foods
28-42 days	20-100	Newly hatched brineshrimp; finely powdered dried foods
40-70 days	20-60	Newly hatched brineshrimp; finely powdered dried foods
About 70 days	20-80	Newly hatched brineshrimp; finely powdered dried foods
60-70 days	30-200	Newly hatched brineshrimp; finely powdered dried foods
40-45 days	Usually 10-20	Newly hatched brineshrimp; finely powdered dried foods

Coldwater fishes

Keeping coldwater fishes in indoor aquariums is, perhaps, almost as popular as keeping tropical species. Many of the commonly kept coldwater fishes are probably a little more hardy than most tropicals, yet no less interesting or attractive to behold behind the glass.

Inmates for the coldwater aquarium include some fishes that are better known as 'tropicals', such as Guppies, some barbs, White Cloud Mountain Minnows and the robust Paradisefish (*Macropodus opercularis*). A range of native European and North American fishes can also be kept in suitable aquariums. Here, we deal with that most ubiquitous of aquarium fishes, the Goldfish, together with the Bitterling, the North American Sunfishes and the hardy Stickleback.

Goldfish

The history of the Goldfish (*Carassius auratus*) dates back 1500 years to China, where it was bred from naturally occurring, but less colourful, native carp. Since then, the Goldfish has been selectively bred into at least 120 strains. The line breeding of strains of fancy Goldfishes is quite specialized, although common Goldfishes are easy to breed if kept correctly, and just as rewarding.

Goldfish can mature in their second summer, but this will depend on a number of factors, including diet, temperature and other environmental influences. Generally speaking, fish older than four or five years should not be used for breeding, since they are probably past their prime.

The breeding season of Goldfishes in temperate regions is from spring to midsummer. At this time the body of the mature female will take on a full, rounded appearance, especially when viewed from above. The mature male develops pale tubercles – small bumps a little like white spot cysts – on the head, gill covers and pectoral fins. This makes the male rough to the touch and he does, in fact, use these to rub up against the female during his courtship manoeuvres.

The sexing of Goldfishes can be confirmed by their behaviour at spawning time; the males will actively chase the female for several days before spawning begins. Outside their breeding season, Goldfishes are difficult to sex. Reputable dealers can, however, supply previously sexed pairs at most times of the year.

Correct care is, of course, vital for successful breeding. This means that in the late summer to autumn in the year before breeding, the fishes must be fed a good varied diet of high-quality prepared foods, along with occasional feeds of safe live foods such as earthworms. Furthermore, as temperatures rise in the spring of the following year, the appetites of the prospective parents should again be tempted with the above foods, but take care to avoid overfeeding and pond or aquarium pollution.

The easiest way to breed Goldfishes is in a garden pond, and in many situations Goldfishes will do so if left to their own devices. For breeding purposes, the pond should have a gently shelving area starting at about 20 to 25cm (8-10in) deep and then gently sloping up to the water surface

Below: Goldfishes can be bred very easily in a pond, but it is advisable to take measures to protect the eggs and fry from their parents. Either separate off the spawning area with fine-mesh netting once the eggs have been laid or remove egg-laden plants to rearing tanks of pond water.

at the pond edge. In the early spring, place bunches of fine-leaved oxygenating plants, such as Milfoil (*Myriophyllum*), Hornwort (*Ceratophyllum*) and Willow Moss (*Fontinalis*), on the shelf in such a way that they can be easily removed after spawning. One way of doing this is to tie the plant bunches to pieces of thread attached to a small stake at the edge of the pond. Goldfish spawning mats are also available from water garden specialists.

When the water temperature reaches about 15°C (59°F), the mature male fishes will begin chasing the females. This often occurs in spring to early summer, depending on where you live. The fish very often spawn early in the morning and continue to do so for several hours. If spawning appears to have taken place, inspect the plants for eggs, which appear as tiny pinhead blobs of jelly scattered singly over the leaves.

If spawning has occurred, transfer the plants to tanks of pond water or to the shallow area of the pond divided off with boards or netting. Since spawning may recur throughout the summer, it is probably better to follow the first option and replace any removed plants with fresh ones.

Goldfishes are avid egg and fry eaters, and other pond inmates, such as other fishes, snails and insects, may also eat the eggs and fry. Therefore, while some eggs and fry will survive if left to their own devices in the pond, a better percentage survival will be obtained if the egg-laden plants are removed to a separate tank or tanks.

In the absence of a pond, or if more controlled conditions are required, it is quite possible to spawn Goldfishes in indoor tanks. Set up a breeding tank not less than 60×30×38cm (24×12×15in) in size, (preferably

Below: *As water temperatures approach 15°C (59°F) in the spring, spawning activity will be seen among mature pond Goldfishes. Spawning may extend through the summer and well into the autumn in a good year.*

larger) in an unheated room. Site it where it can receive some early morning sunshine. Include numerous bunches of fine-leaved plants, but gravel on the tank floor is unnecessary. Provide filtration and aeration with one or more foam filters and use a tight-fitting cover.

Many breeders place their brood stock into the breeding tanks in early spring, with the mature male on one side and the mature female on the other side of a perforated tank divider bisecting the tank into equal halves. As the water temperature creeps above 15°C (59°F), preferably during some sunny weather, reduce the water depth one evening to about 10-12.5cm (4-5in) and remove the partition from the tank.

Spawning should occur the next morning. If not, leave the fish together for a few days. If they still do not spawn, refill the tank with water and replace the partition. Repeat the process about 7-10 days later. In order to induce reluctant fishes to spawn, experience shows that slightly cooling the pond or aquarium water by adding fresh tapwater, or improving the aeration, may bring the desired results. As soon as spawning has occurred in the aquarium, remove the parent fishes.

Set up hatching and rearing tanks for the eggs and fry as described for the spawning tank. Use a heater-thermostat to maintain a steady temperature of 18-20°C (64-68°F), and keep the water depth at this stage at about 10-12.5cm (4-5in).

Above: *To breed Goldfishes in tanks, condition a mature male and female fish ready for spawning on either side of a perforated tank divider. Position the tank in an unheated room where it will receive early morning sunshine and provide suitable filtration.*

The eggs should hatch after three to four days, but the tiny fry will be difficult to see. The fry will survive for approximately 48 hours on their yolk sac reserves. Thereafter, offer them small but frequent meals of green water, infusorians, liquid fry food, newly hatched brineshrimp and finely powdered dry foods. Chopped and ground earthworms make another useful food for the growing fishes.

If the tank is illuminated for 24 hours a day, and the fish are offered four or five feeds daily, they will grow rapidly. However, good filtration and weekly partial water changes of 25 percent are very important. All new water should, of course, be treated with a conditioner. After about a week or two of feeding, top up the tank with conditioned tapwater. By three to four weeks of age the fry should be feeding readily on powdered dry foods and crushed flakes.

At about six weeks of age, when they are 2-3cm (0.8-1.2in) long, the fry will probably need to be thinned out. This is a good time to select the best fishes and pass on the others to friends or local pet stores. Some aquarists use such surplus stock available at this stage as live food for predatory fishes such as cichlids.

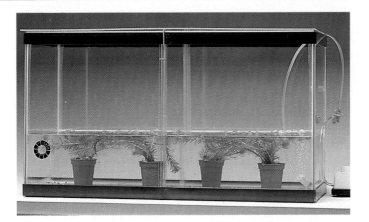

Above: *Goldfishes usually spawn as water temperatures rise in the spring, but to spur things along in a tank set-up, lower the water level and decrease the temperature a little before taking out the partition. Remove the adults after spawning.*

At this time, a stocking level of about 15-20 fish per 60cm (24in) tank is advisable, and will allow them to develop properly. It is a serious mistake to try and rear too many of

the fry, because overcrowding will suppress their growth rate and cause other problems too.

When the fishes are about 5-6cm (2-2.4in) long and six months old, they may begin to turn from a bronze brown to the more characteristic gold colour. Do not winter fish smaller than this in outdoor pools, but keep them inside in tanks until the following spring. Some of the fishes may not change colour until they are at least 12 months old; some never do.

Below: *Fancy Goldfishes (Shubunkins) at four weeks of age. Around this time, or a little later, select the best and dispose of deformed or slow-growing fishes.*

Below: *These eight-week old Shubunkins are just showing their colour patterns. The timing of this change may depend on temperature, diet and the quality of the parents.*

Bitterling

Like the Goldfish, and the barbs and danios described on pages 84-91, the Bitterling (*Rhodeus amarus*) is another member of the cyprinid or carp family. The Bitterling, of which several different species are known, is an interesting little fish that occurs over much of Europe, and has been introduced into several countries. It is normally found in slow-moving rivers and shallow lakes and ponds. The Bitterling has a slim, rather compressed body for a member of the carp family, and normally reaches a maximum length of approximately 9-10cm (3.5-4in).

It is easy to care for. While aeration is not essential in most home aquariums, it is advisable. Keep one male and one or two females in a small tank, at a temperature not

Above: *The strikingly coloured male Bitterling. A number of related* Rhodeus *species are now available; telling them apart is not easy.*

exceeding 20-22°C (68-72°F). The tank should be well planted with such plants as *Elodea* and *Vallisneria*, and the fish fed on a selection of safe live and dried foods. The Bitterling will also live in a garden pond, but will be seldom seen once introduced.

Below: *A unique relationship exists between the Bitterling and the freshwater mussel. It is now thought that the female actually inserts her ovipositor into the exhalant siphon of the mussel, with the milt from the male being drawn in by the mollusc's 'breathing' movements. The eggs are fertilized within the mussel.*

During the spring to early summer breeding season, the male takes on a splendid appearance. A shiny blue-green stripe extends along the sides of the fish, and pale tubercles develop on the head and upper lip. The fins take on a vivid hue, and the throat turns orange-red. While the female is somewhat less striking, both sexes have an overall iridescent sheen to their bodies at this time.

As with many fish from temperate regions, successfully breeding the Bitterling in aquariums requires a drop in temperature – to about 10°C (50°F) or less – during the winter. The Bitterling also needs one or more live freshwater mussels (*Anodonta* sp. or *Unio* sp.) in the tank. In the absence of a mussel, the male and female fish will often refuse to enter into breeding condition, which reflects the unique relationship that exists between the fish and the mollusc.

During the breeding season, the male will swim around its selected mussel, defending it against intruders. During this time, the female develops a short egg tube, or ovipositor, which extends about 1cm (0.4in) from her belly. As a part of courtship, the male guides the female to the mussel, as the ovipositor extends to 4-5cm (1.6-2in) in length. This she inserts into the mollusc and sheds several eggs. The male then sheds his milt, which the mussel draws in by its normal 'breathing' movements. This process is repeated several times.

One female deposits 50 or more eggs, which hatch after two to three weeks. The young fishes spend several days inside the mussel, during which time they are absorbing their yolk sacs. When they emerge, they are free swimming and will feed on small brineshrimp and finely powdered dried foods.

It is interesting to note that in part payment for receiving protection for its eggs and very young fry, the Bitterling (in addition to other fishes) acts as host for the larval stages of the mollusc, the so-called 'glochidia'. These small mussels attach to the skin, gills, and other parts of the fish, where they do little harm unless present in very large numbers.

Sunfishes

The freshwater sunfishes, or centrarchids, form a group of about 30 species of cichlid-like fishes; they are also known as bluegills, crappies and basses. They are native to eastern North America, although a number of species have now been introduced into Europe. They typically live in clear, lowland rivers and lakes, particularly those which are weedy and have a sandy bottom.

The sunfishes range in size from about 3 or 4cm (1.2-1.6in) up to 60cm (24in) or more, although the larger species are of more interest to sport fishermen than to aquarists. However, certain members of the *Lepomis* genus, for example, have attracted the attention of fishkeepers, and although they may be kept in outdoor pools in some areas, they will be seen at their best in an indoor unheated aquarium, where they may also breed successfully.

Many of the sunfishes are rather aggressive and are best kept in a species aquarium with other similarly sized fish. Even then the tank should not be overcrowded. Sunfishes will eat all kinds of live and fresh foods, including earthworms, small fishes, lean raw meat, as well as frozen or freeze-dried foods. Their healthy appetite means that good filtration and regular partial water changes are vital for tank hygiene.

Sunfishes such as the 12-15cm (4.7-6in) Pumpkinseed (*Lepomis gibbosus*) require relatively large aquariums – in the order of 60-100cm (24-39in) – that are well-aerated and filtered. Furnish such a tank with a sandy substrate, one or two smooth-edged rocks and clumps of hardy plants, such as *Vallisneria*, *Elodea* and *Fontinalis* (coldwater Willow Moss). These are widely available.

In order to breed the Pumpkinseed, introduce a pair into an aquarium set up along the lines described above. The Pumpkinseed matures at about two or three years of age and, as with many sunfishes, the male is more colourful than the female. He usually has five to eight pearly to green-blue bands on his flanks, along with orange-red spots on the head and throat. To encourage sunfishes to breed in the aquarium, subject them to an autumn-winter drop in temperature to below 10°C (50°F), followed by a spring rise to normal room temperature.

The spring to early summer is typically the natural breeding season for sunfishes. The male excavates a shallow nest on the tank floor and then attracts the female to it. The pair then circle the nest and eventually the female deposits her eggs, which are then fertilized by the male. The female may lay from several hundred to several thousand sticky eggs, and afterwards she is driven away by the male. Remove her from the aquarium at this point.

The eggs are tended and guarded by the male and hatch after three to five days. The tiny fry stay in or around the nest for a few days after this. They then become free swimming and should be offered newly hatched brineshrimp and similar fry foods. The male continues to protect the brood for a period of two weeks or so. By then the 'family' will be seen to be dispersing and the young should be removed, reared on in a separate tank and fed the same wide range of foods that the parent fishes enjoy.

Above: *The 'ear-flap' (an extension to the gill cover) is characteristic of the Pumpkinseed, Lepomis gibbosus. Male sunfishes are generally more colourful than the females.*

Three-spined Stickleback

The Three-spined Stickleback (*Gasterosteus aculeatus*) is a common inhabitant of lakes, rivers and streams over much of northern Europe, where it often appears to occur when pollution has removed more sensitive fish species. It grows to 5-8cm (2-3.2in) in length and is the fish that most youngsters bring home in a jam jar from a local pond or stream. Given the correct care, it is quite possible to keep and breed this fish in the aquarium, where it will exhibit spawning behaviour and brood care very similar to the American sunfishes.

Below: *The Pumpkinseed is a beautifully marked, but a little aggressive, coldwater fish. Keep it in a species aquarium or a large community tank of similar-sized fish.*

The simplest way to breed sticklebacks is to obtain a male and two or three females in the early spring. Introduce these into a 60cm (24in) unheated indoor aquarium containing a substrate of fine gravel, one or two rocks and some clumps of fine-leaved plants, such as *Myriophyllum* and *Fontinalis*. Filter and aerate the tank water using a foam filter, and feed the fishes regularly on a varied diet of live foods and good-quality flaked foods.

The mature male fish, easily distinguishd by his bright red throat, should soon build a nest of plant fragments on the tank floor, and begin displaying to the less brightly coloured, more rounded female. The male will eventually lead one of the females into the nest, where she will lay her 100 or so eggs. The male may mate with more than one female, and he then religiously tends and guards the nest. The male is particularly aggressive at this time, attacking all intruders into his territory, especially other male sticklebacks. For this reason, sticklebacks are best bred in a species aquarium, with no more than one male per tank. This will produce the best chances of success.

Above: *The tank set-up for breeding sticklebacks can be very simple. Although not essential, good filtration is to be recommended.*

Below: *A pair of Three-spined Sticklebacks,* Gasterosteus aculeatus. *Note the red belly and blue eyes of the male. Despite its small size, the male stickleback can be very aggressive at breeding time.*

The fry hatch after seven or eight days at 17-18°C (63-64°F) – longer at lower temperatures – and the young fry can be fed on newly hatched brineshrimp and sieved *Daphnia*. The fry are guarded by the male stickleback until they finally leave his protection after a week or two. Rear the young fishes on using a good varied diet. Although the main breeding season is in spring, sticklebacks will often continue to breed until mid to late summer.

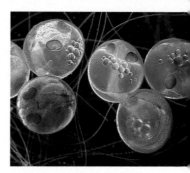

Above right: *Fish eggs, (in this case sticklebacks) with developing embryos are termed 'eyed', from the visible eyes of the would-be fry. The fry emerge after seven or eight days.*

Right: *Spawning Three-spined Sticklebacks at the nest. The male often mates with several females and then cares for the eggs and young fry until they are a week or two old.*

BREEDING TABLE – COLDWATER FISHES

FISH SPECIES	SEXUAL CHARACTERISTICS	WATER CONDITIONS FOR BREEDING
Goldfish (Carassius auratus)	Female more rounded; male with spawning 'tubercles'	Spring rise to 15°C (59°F); avoid extremes of pH and hardness
Bitterling (Rhodeus amarus)	Male more colourful; female with long 'egg tube' at breeding time	Spring rise in temperature; avoid extremes of pH and hardness; presence of mussel important for breeding
Pumpkinseed (Lepomis gibbosus)	Male more colourful than female	Spring rise in temperature; avoid extremes of pH and harness
Three-spined Stickleback (Gasterosteus aculeatus)	Male with red throat; female more rounded	Obtain mature fishes in spring and maintain at ambient temperature

SPAWNING METHOD AND BROOD CARE	NUMBER OF EGGS AND HATCHING TIME	FIRST FOOD FOR FRY
Eggs laid among plants or spawning 'mats'; remove parents or eggs once spawning is complete	Many thousands of eggs; 3-4 days to hatch	Green water; infusorians; liquid fry food
Eggs laid into mussel; emerge as small fry	50 or so eggs; 2-3 weeks to hatch	Newly hatched brineshrimp; finely powdered dried foods
Male constructs a nest, and guards nest, eggs and fry	Several thousand eggs; 3-5 days to hatch	Newly hatched brineshrimp; finely powdered dried foods
Male constructs nest, and guards nest, eggs and fry	100 or so eggs; about a week to hatch	Newly hatched brineshrimp

Index to fishes and plants

Page numbers in bold indicate major references, including accompanying photographs. Page numbers in *italics* indicate captions to other illustrations. Less important text entries are in normal type.

Further Reading

Books

Adams T. and K. Bannister, *Aquarial fish* Frederick Muller Ltd

Amlacher E., *Textbook of Fish Diseases* T.F.H. Publications

Axelrod H. et al, *Exotic Tropical Fishes* T.F.H. Publications, looseleaf edition

Baensch U., *Tropical Aquarium Fish* Tetra Press

Bryant, P., K. Jauncey and T. Atack, *Backyard Fish Farming* Prism Press

Hervey G.F. and J. Hems, *The Goldfish* Faber

Lowe-McConnell R.H., *Fish Communities in Tropical Freshwaters* Longman Group

Masters C.O., *Encyclopedia of Live Foods* T.F.H. Publications

Mills D. and G. Vevers, *The Practical Encyclopedia of Freshwater Tropical Aquarium Fishes* Salamander Books

Moyle P.M. and J.J. Cech, *Fishes – an Introduction to Ichthyology* Prentice-Hall

Muus B. and P. Dahlstrom, *Collins Guide to Freshwater Fishes of Britain and Europe* Collins

Ostermoller, W., *Fish Breeding Recipes* T.F.H. Publications

van Ramshorst J.D., *The Complete Aquarium Encyclopedia of Tropical Freshwater Fish* Phaidon

Sagar K., *World Encyclopedia of Tropical Fish* Octopus

Sterba G., *The Aquarists Encyclopedia* Blandford Press

Varley M.E., *British Freshwater Fishes* Fishing News (Books) Ltd

Whitehead P., *How Fishes Live* Phaidon

Magazines

Aquarist and Pondkeeper Buckley Press, Half acre, Brentford TW8 8BN, England

Aquarium Digest Tetra, 201 Tabor Road, Morris Plains, N.J. 07950, U.S.A.

Freshwater and Marine Aquarium Magazine P.O. Box 487, Sierra Madre, California 91024, U.S.A.

Practical Fishkeeping EMAP National Publications, Bretton Court, Bretton, Peterborough PE3 8DZ, England

Tropical Fish Hobbyist 211 W. Sylvania Avenue, Neptune City, N.J. 07753, U.S.A.

Companion volumes of interest:

A Fishkeeper's Guide to THE TROPICAL AQUARIUM

A Fishkeeper's Guide to COMMUNITY FISHES

A Fishkeeper's Guide to COLDWATER FISHES

A Fishkeeper's Guide to MARINE FISHES

A Fishkeeper's Guide to MAINTAINING A HEALTHY AQUARIUM

A Fishkeeper's Guide to GARDEN PONDS

A Fishkeeper's Guide to AQUARIUM PLANTS

A Fishkeeper's Guide to CENTRAL AMERICAN CICHLIDS

A Petkeeper's Guide to REPTILES AND AMPHIBIANS

Picture Credits

Artists
Copyright of the artwork illustrations on the pages following the artists' names is the property of Salamander Books Ltd.

Janos Marffy: 23, 24, 25, 27, 104

Clifford and Wendy Meadway: 22, 26

Photographs
The publishers wish to thank the following photographers and agencies who have supplied photographs for this book. The photographs have been credited by page number and position on the page: (B) Bottom, (T) Top, (C) Centre, (BL) Bottom left etc.

David Allison: 110(B)

Dr. Chris Andrews: 21, 30(T), 33(T), 35(T)

Heather Angel/Biofotos: 111(B)

Bruce Coleman: 43(T, Jane Burton), 100 (Jane Burton), 112 (Kim Taylor)

Eric Crichton © Salamander Books Ltd: 13(T)

Jan Eric Larsson: 31(T), 32(T), 34, 41(T), 49(T), 48-9, 79, 96, 101(C)

Dick Mills: 35(BR), 40, 44-5

Arend van den Nieuwenhuizen: Title page, 52, 60-1(B), 62, 67, 70(B), 89(B), 90(T), 93, 94, 95, 98(T)

Laurence Perkins: 47, 105

Mike Sandford: Half-title, 38-9, 41(B), 70(T), 108(T), 110(T)

David Sands: 30(B)

Peter W. Scott: 33(TR)

W. Tomey: 53(T)

Dr. Jörg Vierke: 14, 15, 60(C), 63, 73

Keith Waller Associates © Salamander Books Ltd: 12-13, 13(B), 16, 18, 19, 20, 28, 35(BL), 43(B), 48(T), 50-1, 54-5, 58-9(B), 66, 71, 72, 76-7(B), 80, 84-5(B), 87(T), 89(T), 92, 97, 99(B), 101(B), 106, 107(T), 111(T)

Pam Whittington: 107(B)

Lothar Wischnath: 113(T)

Rudolf Zukal: Endpapers, Copyright page, 38-9, 50(T), 53(C,B), 55(T), 56, 57, 59(T), 60(T), 62(T), 68, 69, 74, 75, 76(T), 77(T), 78, 81, 83, 85, 86, 87(B), 88, 99

Georg Zurlo: 10-11, 27, 108(B)

Author's acknowledgements
The author wishes to thank Tetra (UK), expecially Mrs. C. Short; Shelley Couper; and Ken and Dot Overment at the Bath Pet Shop for their help in preparing the book.

PRINTED IN BELGIUM BY

INTERNATIONAL BOOK PRODUCTION

Xiphophorus variatus *(Variatus Platy)*